minutemeals

D1368635

3 ways to dinner

new ideas for favorite main-dish ingredients

Edited by Evie Righter

Wiley Publishing, Inc.

Library of Congress Cataloging-in-Publication Data
Minutemeals 3 ways to dinner : 20-minute gourmet menus /
        edited by Evie Righter.
            p. cm.
        ISBN 0-7645-6609-1 (pbk. : alk. paper)
        1. Quick and easy cookery.   2. Menus.   I. Righter, Evie.
II. Title: Minutemeals three ways to dinner.
TX833.5.M555 2002
641.5'55—dc21

2002008220

minutemeals

Joe Langhan, President, minutemeals.com Inc.

Miriam Garron, Managing Editor

Miriam Rubin, Consulting Food Editor

Cover design by Edwin Kuo

Interior design by Edwin Kuo

Cover photographs David Bishop

Manufactured in the United States of America

10   9   8   7   6   5   4   3   2   1

welcome to the third book, *3 ways to dinner,*

in the minutemeals series of cookbooks. By this time, we hope you have discovered minutemeals, if not from our web site, minutemeals.com, then from our two recent titles: the first, *minutemeals, 20-minute gourmet menus,* and the second, *minutemeals vegetarian.*

if you already use our cookbooks or web site, you know that a delicious home-cooked meal is doable in only 20 minutes. If you are new to the concept, here it is in a nutshell: We know that time for almost everything, but especially for cooking, is short. We also know that home-cooked wins out over order-in or take-out any day. Home-cooked, though, can often mean a large investment of time, which nobody has.

we found the fix, and it's not fast food or opening a can. It is minutemeals, home-cooked meals that take only 20 minutes to make. We provide the menu, the shopping and pantry ingredients lists, and the organizational roadmap, known as the "menu gameplan," so that you can concentrate on just the preparation of the meal. There is no easier way to go from the idea of a tasty home-cooked dinner to actually serving that freshly made dinner to your family than a minutemeal menu.

which brings us to the 81 menus here. How often has the harried cook heard: "Chicken, again?" or "We had spaghetti Monday night, Mom." The same old food gets very old, very fast, in most households. So much for the tried-and-true, but what to do about it?

open up *3 ways to dinner,* and relax. We've selected 27 popular foods, main-course protein items mostly, and created 3 totally different menus for each. This is how it works: You have beef for stir-fry in the refrigerator for dinner. You could make your standard recipe—again—and watch the family push all that hard work of yours around on the plate. Or you could choose from among our (1) *Sesame Garlic Beef* menu, or (2) our *Beef Fajitas* menu, or (3) our *Sloppy Joes* menu. Three ways, each different. Remember that not only are you getting a different recipe for the same food item, you are getting a complete menu that is totally different as well.

if what to make for dinner has been a problem, it doesn't have to be anymore, not when you can rely on *3 ways to dinner* for inspiration. Imagine, variety *and* memorable home-cooked meals, otherwise known as minutemeals, in only 20 minutes.

Evie Righter, Editor

minutemeals
3 ways to dinner

meet the minutemeals chefs

We'd like you to meet the chefs behind minutemeals, the people whose creativity and ingenuity created the delicious menus in this book. Their combined expertise is our ace in the hole—the secret that keeps our menus fresh, interesting, and full of great ideas. You'll find their helpful comments throughout the book, paired with the menus they created.

Ruth Fisher
Miriam Garron
Marge Perry
Paul Piccuito
Sarah Reynolds
Hillary Davis Tonken

how to use this book

minutemeals 3 ways to dinner is designed to be as efficient as possible. Twenty minutes, after all, is a short amount of time to cook a full meal and place it on the table. For you to be able to do the cooking with as few setbacks as possible, we took care of as many of the time-consuming details as we could to ensure your success. Rely on our system and you will have a delicious dinner on the table in 20 minutes.

Each menu includes a shopping list of the major ingredients needed, as well as a complete list of ingredients we consider standard pantry items. No more hunting through multiple recipes to glean what you need to buy on the way home—we've done that for you. Our "menu gameplan" then orders the sequence of just how to go about cooking the meal—what dish needs to be started first, what should follow, and so on. We've also noted when to preheat the oven or broiler so that it will be sufficiently heated for maximum cooking results. The double-page format of each menu guarantees that when you refer to the cooking directions of any given dish you are always on the "same page."

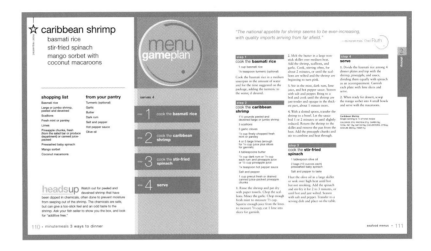

This book provides great new ideas and options for your favorite main-dish ingredients. Did you stock up on chicken breasts, ground beef, or canned tuna? Then you'll love the fact that there are 3 complete and very different menus for each ingredient. Keep buying what you like—minutemeals will help you make it taste different and good. To identify a main ingredient effortlessly, *without* referring to the index, just look for the vertical heading in the margin of each righthand page.

The minutemeals clock starts ticking when you put the ingredients for a menu on the kitchen counter. The first several times you make a menu expect it to take a few minutes more than you had anticipated: the system itself and the recipes are new to you and, as the saying goes, practice makes perfect. Once you've had the practice, we know that you will find the results satisfying . . . and quick.

quick tips from the pros

sara moulton

creative ways with intentional leftovers

mix a big batch of vinaigrette, not just for salads, but also for sauces and marinades. I mix 3 parts oil with 1 part vinegar and add flavoring to taste as I use it: I'll add fresh or dried herbs to make a marinade; or swirl some vinaigrette into pan drippings from chicken cutlets, and then add mustard, fresh or dried herbs, garlic, lemon zest, olive paste, or sun-dried tomatoes to make a pan sauce.

bake potatoes over the weekend and use them for home fries and hash. I use them in potato soup: I add peeled, diced potatoes, chopped leeks, and fresh herbs to stock, and then purée. Sometimes I add milk or cream at this point, or garnish with a dollop of sour cream.

make double batches of thin pasta and use leftovers for "pasta pizza": Rinse the extra pasta in cold water; drain. Transfer to a self-sealing bag and refrigerate for up to two days or freeze for up to one month. To cook, heat olive oil in a nonstick skillet over medium high heat, add the pasta, and cook until the bottom is crisp. Flip it, crisp the other side, then top with marinara sauce, cheese, and your favorite toppings.

have on hand a good supply of canned, bottled, and dry ingredients with intense flavors. Good-quality canned tomatoes, tuna, and capers, for example, make a quick and easy sauce for pasta.

Sara Moulton is the star of Food Network's *Cooking Live* and *Sara's Secrets,* the on-air food editor at *Good Morning America,* and *Gourmet* magazine's executive chef, a position she has held for 15 years. Her first cookbook, *Sara Moulton Cooks at Home,* will be published in October, 2002. A graduate of the Culinary Institute of America, Sara studied in France and cooked in Boston and New York prior to her television and magazine career. In 1982 Sara co-founded the New York Women's Culinary Alliance to promote cooperation and education among women in the food industry.

nick stellino

easier, faster pasta? it's possible

even I keep a jar of my favorite prepared tomato sauce in the pantry for emergencies. To give it a home-made touch, I sauté chopped sausage (hot or sweet) with some sliced onions and chopped garlic until the sausage is golden brown; then I add the sauce and simmer for 15 minutes.

believe it or not, you can cook pasta one day ahead, a good trick to know when you are entertaining and need to save time. Cook the pasta for 3/4 of the recommended cooking time, and then immediately rinse it in cold water to stop the cooking process. Toss it pasta with olive oil—3 to 4 tablespoons per pound of pasta—and refrigerate. When you are ready to serve, plunge the pasta into boiling salted water and cook to al dente—no more! Then drain and sauce as you would normally. This method will work with any pasta except angel hair, which is just too delicate.

even lasagna can be simplified: Try using imported Italian lasagna sheets, which do not require any pre-cooking. I find that I can shave 20 minutes off my preparation time by using the sheets.

Nick Stellino is currently hosting his second year of *Nick Stellino's Family Kitchen II,* which airs on public television. Based on his book *Nick Stellino's Family Passione: Pasta, Pizza, and Pannini,* (Putnam, 2000), the series features the food of Nick's native Sicily. The series premiered in 2000, following the publication of *Nick Stellino's Family Kitchen* cookbook (Putnam, 1999). Nick launched his television career in 1994 with the Mediterranean cooking series *Cucina Amore,* which quickly became one of the most popular food programs on U.S. television, and ultimately was ranked as public television's number one "how-to" series. Nick has also appeared in two PBS culinary specials and is the author of the cookbooks *Cucina Amore, Glorious Italian Cooking,* and *Mediterranean Flavors.*

marge perry

clean and simple

I make a variety of fast, delicious vegetable soups with my immersion (hand-held) blender and just one pot. I simmer vegetables in flavored chicken or vegetable broth until tender, then purée them right in the pot. All of the nutrients and flavors from the vegetables go right into the soup, which has a creamy, frothy texture. And remember—the smaller the vegetable pieces, the faster they cook.

once I drain pasta, I save clean-up by returning it to the now-empty pot to toss with my sauce and other ingredients. I save even more clean-up time—and add valuable nutrients—by cooking frozen peas, spinach, broccoli, cauliflower or other vegetables I have on hand with the pasta in the last few minutes of it's cooking time.

I always have shredded cheese—the kind that comes in resealable bags—on hand for pizza topping, pasta, and salad. I find that once opened, it doesn't keep well in the refrigerator, so I keep it in the freezer—and because it is already shredded, I don't have to thaw it before using. I just grab a handful and add it frozen to whatever I'm cooking. I even add it to salads. I leave it at room temperature while I prepare the rest of the meal; by the time I'm ready to serve dinner, it's thawed.

Marge Perry writes, broadcasts, and teaches about cooking and culinary lifestyle issues such as stress-free entertaining, cultural influences in cooking, health and nutrition, and more. She is a nationally syndicated writer whose newspaper work includes a daily column called *Dinner Tonight* for Newsday and regular feature articles. Marge is a contributing editor for *Cooking Light,* and frequently writes for many national magazines, including *Self, Better Homes and Gardens, Health, InTouch* and more. Her broadcast work includes her long-running weekly television segments called "Meals in a Flash" and "At the Market," and many radio and television appearances. Ms. Perry's book, *Dinner Tonight,* includes close to 150 healthful, fast, complete meals. She is currently at work on two books on entertaining.

minute
3 ways

poultry menus

meals
to dinner

☆ chicken cacciatore

avocado caesar salad with lime
garlic bread
ripe plums or clementines

menu gameplan

shopping list

Mushroom slices
(from the salad bar or produce department)

Skinless boneless chicken breast halves

Frozen garlic bread loaf

Ripe avocado

Caesar salad dressing

Lime (for juice)

Prewashed romaine salad mix

Ripe plums (or clementines)

from your pantry

Onion

Olive oil

Basil-and-tomato marinara sauce

Crushed red pepper flakes

serves 4

beforeyoustart

Preheat the oven to heat the garlic bread. Rinse the plums, if serving.

step 1 — cook the **chicken cacciatore**

step 2 — heat the **garlic bread**

step 3 — assemble the **avocado caesar salad with lime**

step 4 — **serve**

headsup

Cut off the ends of the garlic bread before serving and cut into cubes. Use as warm croutons on your salad. If any garlic bread remains, cube the remainder, toast in the oven until golden, and use as croutons (store airtight).

"Traditional chicken cacciatore cooks in 1½ hours, but I've streamlined this recipe to 16 minutes, without sacrificing the flavor."

—minutemeals' Chef Paul

step 1

cook the **chicken cacciatore**

1 large onion

1 tablespoon olive oil

1 package (8 ounces) sliced mushrooms

1 pound skinless boneless chicken breast halves

1 jar (16 ounces) good-quality basil-and-tomato marinara sauce (about 2 cups)

1/4 teaspoon crushed red pepper flakes

1. Coarsely chop the onion.

2. Place the oil in a large nonstick skillet over high heat. Add the onion and mushrooms and cook, stirring often, for 5 minutes, or until the onion is tender.

3. Meanwhile, cut the chicken breasts into 1-inch chunks.

4. Push the vegetables aside, add the chicken and cook, turning the pieces often, for 3 to 4 minutes, until the chicken is lightly browned.

5. Add the marinara sauce and pepper flakes, reduce the heat to medium, and simmer for 5 to 6 minutes, or until chicken is cooked through.

step 2

heat the **garlic bread**

1 loaf (about 16 ounces) frozen garlic bread

1. Preheat the oven according to the directions on the bread package.

2. Bake the bread for the time suggested, transfer it to a napkin-lined basket, and cover to keep warm.

step 3

assemble the **avocado caesar salad with lime**

1 ripe avocado

1/3 cup store-bought Caesar salad dressing

1 tablespoon fresh lime juice (1 lime)

1 bag (5 ounces) prewashed romaine salad mix

1. Halve, pit, and peel the avocado; cut into cubes.

2. Combine the dressing and lime juice in a salad bowl. Add the avocado and toss gently until coated with dressing. Place the romaine on top; do not toss until serving.

step 4

serve

1. Divide the chicken cacciatore among 4 dinner plates.

2. Place the garlic bread on the table.

3. Toss the salad and top with garlic bread cubes, if using. Serve.

4. When ready for dessert, arrange the fruit in a bowl. Place on the table with 4 dessert plates.

Chicken Cacciatore
Single serving is 1/4 of total recipe
CALORIES 246; PROTEIN 27g; CARBS 15g; TOTAL FAT 9g; SAT FAT 2g; CHOLESTEROL 63mg; SODIUM 525mg; FIBER 3g

☆ sesame lemon chicken

coconut brown rice with spinach

brownies or blondies

menu gameplan

serves 4

shopping list

Instant brown rice

Lite coconut milk
(in Asian or Spanish
foods section)

Frozen chopped spinach
(in a bag)

Lemon (for zest and juice)

Skinless boneless
chicken breast halves

Gingerroot

Scallions

Sliced water chestnuts

Sweet-and-sour sauce

Sesame seeds

Brownies or blondies

from your pantry

Chinese 5-spice powder or
ground allspice (optional)

Peanut or vegetable oil

Toasted sesame oil

step **1** cook the **coconut brown rice with spinach**

step **2** make the **sesame lemon chicken**

step **3** **serve**

headsup

Sweet-and-sour sauce is sold in the Asian section of your supermarket. If you can't find it, substitute an equal amount of duck sauce, apricot jam, or apple jelly.

"Chill the rice mixture, then add grilled shrimp, diced mango, and citrus salad dressing and you have a great main-course summer meal."

—minutemeals' Chef Paul

step 1

cook the **coconut brown rice with spinach**

1 cup instant brown rice

1/2 cup lite coconut milk

1 cup frozen chopped spinach

1/8 teaspoon Chinese 5-spice powder or ground allspice (optional)

1. Prepare the brown rice according to the directions on the package, adding the coconut milk and reducing the recommended water by 1/4 cup.

2. Stir in the spinach and 5-spice power, if using, during the last 4 minutes of cooking. Remove the pan from the heat and keep warm, covered.

step 2

make the **sesame lemon chicken**

1 large lemon

1 1/2 pounds skinless boneless chicken breast halves

1-inch slice fresh gingerroot

4 scallions

1 tablespoon peanut or vegetable oil

1 can (8 ounces) drained sliced water chestnuts

1/3 cup sweet-and-sour sauce

2 tablespoons sesame seeds

2 teaspoons toasted sesame oil

1. Grate the zest on the lemon. Halve the lemon and juice (2 tablespoons needed). Cut the chicken breasts crosswise on the diagonal into strips. Place the chicken, lemon zest, and 1 tablespoon of the lemon juice in a bowl and toss. Peel the ginger and chop it. Slice scallions in 1-inch lengths.

2. Heat the peanut or vegetable oil in a wok or large nonstick skillet or Dutch oven over high heat until hot but not smoking. Add the chicken and cook, tossing frequently, for 5 minutes. Add the ginger, scallions, and water chestnuts, and cook, stirring, for 1 minute.

3. Stir in the sweet-and-sour sauce, sesame seeds, sesame oil, and remaining 1 tablespoon lemon juice and heat until bubbly. Remove the pan from the heat.

step 3

serve

1. Ladle the rice to the side on 4 dinner plates. Spoon the chicken mixture beside the rice, dividing it evenly.

2. When ready for dessert, cut the brownies or blondies into bars and serve on a plate.

Sesame Lemon Chicken
Single serving is 1/4 of total recipe
CALORIES 316; PROTEIN 35g; CARBS 14g;
TOTAL FAT 10g; SAT FAT 2g; CHOLESTEROL 94mg;
SODIUM 216mg; FIBER 3g

☆ broiled chicken
with apricot glaze

micro-baked sweet potatoes

asparagus with shallot butter

orange sherbet and
butter cookies

menu
gameplan

shopping list

Sweet potatoes

Asparagus

Shallots

Lemon (for juice)

Apricot preserves or
orange marmalade

Skinless boneless
chicken breast halves

Orange sherbet

Chocolate-dipped
butter cookies

from your pantry

Butter

Salt and pepper

Nonstick vegetable
cooking spray

Ketchup

Cider vinegar

Dried thyme

serves 4

beforeyoustart
Preheat the broiler.

step **1** cook the **micro-baked sweet potatoes**

step **2** cook the **asparagus with shallot butter**

step **3** make the **broiled chicken with apricot glaze**

step **4** **serve**

luckyforyou
Only 5 ingredients go into making this chicken entree and with any luck at all you will have at least 3 of them on hand as staples.

"The calories per serving are great, the colors are beautiful, the flavors are clear—there's a lot to like in this quick menu."

—minutemeals' Chef Paul

step 1

cook the **micro-baked sweet potatoes**

4 small sweet potatoes
(or 2 large)

Butter for serving

Salt and pepper to taste

1. Scrub the sweet potatoes and prick in several places with a fork or skewer.

2. Place a piece of paper towel in the microwave and arrange the potatoes like the spokes of a wheel on the towel. Microwave on High for 13 to 17 minutes for 4 potatoes, a little less for 2 potatoes, turning them over once and giving each a quarter turn twice while cooking. Microwave until the potatoes yield a bit to pressure when squeezed. Let stand a few minutes to finish cooking before serving to soften.

step 2

cook the **asparagus with shallot butter**

1 pound thin asparagus

2 shallots

3 tablespoons butter

1 tablespoon fresh lemon juice

Salt and pepper to taste

1. Trim the asparagus, if necessary.

2. Fill a large skillet with 1 inch of water, cover, and bring to a boil over high heat. Add the asparagus,

bring the water back to a boil, and simmer for 4 to 6 minutes, or until just crisp-tender. Drain and transfer to a serving platter.

3. Thinly slice the shallots.

4. In the same skillet, melt the butter over medium heat about 1 minute, or until just beginning to brown. Add the shallots and cook, stirring, for 1 minute until softened. Swirl in the lemon juice and season with salt and pepper. Pour the shallot butter over the asparagus. Cover to keep warm.

step 3

make the **broiled chicken with apricot glaze**

Nonstick vegetable cooking spray

3 tablespoons apricot preserves or orange marmalade

1 tablespoon ketchup

1/2 teaspoon cider vinegar

4 skinless boneless chicken breast halves (5 to 6 ounces), trimmed

1/2 teaspoon crumbled dried thyme

Salt and pepper to taste

1. Preheat the broiler. Line the broiler pan with aluminum foil. Spray the broiler-pan rack with nonstick vegetable cooking spray.

2. In a cup, stir together the preserves or marmalade, ketchup, and vinegar.

3. Season the chicken breasts with the thyme and salt and pepper. Arrange the chicken breasts, skin side down, on the prepared pan and broil 4 to 6 inches from the heat for 5 minutes. Turn and broil for 3 minutes. Brush each chicken breast with some of the fruit glaze and broil for 1 to 2 minutes, until the glaze is bubbly and the chicken is no longer pink in the thickest part. Remove from the broiler.

step 4

serve

1. Place a chicken breast on each of 4 dinner plates.

2. Add a whole or half sweet potato to each plate and serve with butter and salt and pepper on the table.

3. Place the asparagus on the table.

4. When ready for dessert, scoop the orange sherbet into 4 dessert bowls, garnish each serving with 1 or 2 butter cookies, and serve.

Broiled Chicken with Apricot Glaze
Single serving is 1/4 of total recipe
CALORIES 193; PROTEIN 29g; CARBS 11g;
TOTAL FAT 3g; SAT FAT 1g; CHOLESTEROL 78mg;
SODIUM 270 mg; FIBER 0g

☆ basque chicken
herb-tossed orzo
prune plums and grapes

shopping list

Chicken tenders

Smoked ham

Mixed olives, pitted

Diced tomatoes with
roasted garlic

Orzo

Fresh parsley

Prune plums

Seedless red or green grapes

from the salad bar

Green pepper slices

Onion slices

from your pantry

Olive oil

Salt and pepper

Dried thyme

Butter

serves 4

step	**1**	cook the **basque chicken**
step	**2**	cook the **herb-tossed orzo**
	3	rinse the **prune plums and grapes**
	4	**serve**

headsup
Chicken tenders have a tough tendon running through them, which may not have been removed prior to packaging. If not, cut out the thickest part, visible at one end, with a sharp knife.

"The combination of chicken, ham, tomatoes, onions, peppers, garlic, and olives makes this a classic Basque dish. Be sure to serve it with crusty bread."

—minutemeals' Chef Sarah

step 1

cook the **basque chicken**

2 cups green pepper slices

1 tablespoon olive oil

1 cup onion slices

1 pound chicken tenders

Salt and pepper to taste

1/2 cup diced smoked ham

1/2 cup pitted marinated mixed olives

1 can (14.5 ounces) diced tomatoes with roasted garlic

1/4 cup water

1. Cut the pepper slices in half.

2. In a large deep heavy skillet, heat the olive oil over medium-high heat. Add the green pepper and onion slices. Reduce the heat to medium, cover, and cook, stirring occasionally, for 3 minutes, until the vegetables soften slightly.

3. Meanwhile, cut the chicken tenders into 1 1/2-inch chunks and season lightly with salt and pepper. Dice the smoked ham.

4. Add the olives, chicken, ham, tomatoes, and water to the skillet. Cover and bring to a boil. Reduce the heat and simmer, covered, stirring occasionally, for 8 to 10 minutes, until the chicken is cooked through.

step 2

cook the **herb-tossed orzo**

1 cup orzo

Salt and pepper to taste

1/4 cup lightly packed fresh parsley leaves

1/4 teaspoon crumbled dried thyme

2 tablespoons butter

1. Bring a medium saucepan of water to a boil, covered. Add the orzo and salt and cook according to the directions on the package until *al dente*.

2. While the orzo cooks, chop the parsley.

3. Drain the orzo. Return it to the saucepan and add the herbs and butter. Season with salt and pepper. Stir until the butter has melted.

step 3

rinse the **prune plums and grapes**

8 prune plums

1 medium bunch seedless red or green grapes

Rinse the fruits separately in a colander, then transfer to a serving bowl. Chill, if desired, until serving time.

step 4

serve

1. Divide the chicken and orzo among 4 dinner plates and serve.

2. When ready for dessert, serve the fruit directly from the bowl with 4 dessert plates.

Basque Chicken
Single serving is 1/4 of total recipe
CALORIES 302; PROTEIN 27g; CARBS 17g;
TOTAL Fat 12g; SAT FAT 2g; CHOLESTEROL 69mg;
SODIUM 1142mg; FIBER 3g

☆ louisiana poorboys

cajun roast potatoes

vanilla ice cream with
bananas foster sauce

menu
gameplan

shopping list

Precooked new potato
wedges

Ripe bananas

Vanilla ice cream

Tomatoes

Shredded iceberg lettuce
(from the salad bar)

Chicken tenders

French bread

from your pantry

Olive oil

Cajun or Creole seasoning

Butter

Brown sugar

Orange juice

Rum or bourbon

Ground cinnamon

Mayonnaise

Creole or whole-grain
mustard

Garlic-and-herb seasoning
or garlic salt

serves 4

beforeyoustart

Preheat the oven to 450°F to roast
the potatoes.

step **1** make the **cajun roast potatoes**

step **2** make the **bananas foster sauce**

step **3** prepare the **louisiana poorboys**

step **4** **serve**

luckyforyou Precooked potato wedges
are available in the refriger-
ated foods section of the produce or meat department of
the supermarket.

"New Orleans' great sandwich, the poorboy, is often made with fried oysters or shrimp. Garlicky chicken makes a tasty poorboy, too."

—minutemeals' Chef Sarah

step 1

make the **cajun roast potatoes**

1 bag (1 1/4 pounds) refrigerated precooked new potato wedges

1 tablespoon olive oil

1 teaspoon Cajun or Creole seasoning

1. Preheat the oven to 450°F.

2. On a jelly-roll pan, toss the potatoes with the olive oil and seasoning. Spread in a single layer. Bake for about 10 minutes, or until golden brown.

step 2

make the **bananas foster sauce**

2 medium firm ripe bananas

2 tablespoons butter

1/4 cup packed brown sugar

2 tablespoons orange juice

2 tablespoons rum or bourbon

1/8 teaspoon ground cinnamon

1 pint vanilla ice cream

1. Peel and slice the bananas.

2. In a medium nonstick skillet, heat the butter and brown sugar over medium heat, stirring, until the sugar melts, about 1 minute. Add the bananas and cook, stirring

frequently, until they soften, about 2 minutes. Stir in the orange juice, rum, and cinnamon and bring to a simmer. Remove the skillet from the heat and cover to keep warm.

3. Scoop the ice cream into 4 dessert bowls and place in the freezer.

step 3

prepare the **louisiana poorboys**

2 medium tomatoes

2 cups shredded iceberg lettuce

1/3 cup mayonnaise

1 tablespoon Creole or whole-grain mustard

2 tablespoons olive oil

1 1/4 pounds chicken tenders

1 1/2 teaspoons garlic-and-herb seasoning or garlic salt

1 long loaf French bread

1. Thinly slice the tomatoes. Finely shred the lettuce.

2. In a small bowl, combine the mayonnaise and mustard.

3. In a large heavy skillet, heat the olive oil over medium-high heat. Add the chicken, sprinkle with the garlic-and-herb seasoning, and cook for 5 to 8 minutes, turning once, until lightly browned and no longer pink in the thickest part.

4. Cut the bread in half lengthwise and spread the cut sides with the mustard mayonnaise. Top the bottom half with tomatoes, chicken, and lettuce. Cover with the top half of the bread. Cut the loaf into 4 equal pieces.

step 4

serve

1. Place a piece of the poorboy on each of 4 dinner plates and add Cajun potatoes to each serving, dividing them equally.

2. When ready for dessert, spoon some of the warm banana sauce over the ice cream and serve at once.

Louisiana Poorboys
Single serving is 1/4 of total recipe
CALORIES 614; PROTEIN 37g; CARBS 50g;
TOTAL FAT 27g; SAT FAT 5g; CHOLESTEROL 89mg;
SODIUM 1,860mg; FIBER 4g

☆ asian orange chicken
cashew rice
strawberry ice cream

menu
gameplan

shopping list

Cashews

Scallion

Orange (for zest and juice)

Chicken tenders

Fresh stir-fry vegetables (packaged in the produce department)

Pre-chopped garlic

Pre-minced ginger

Strawberry ice cream

from your pantry

Boil-in-bag rice

Hot chile oil

Salt and pepper

Teriyaki sauce

Cornstarch

Vegetable oil

serves 4

beforeyoustart

Bring 8 cups water to a boil in a medium saucepan, covered, for the rice.

step **1** prepare the **cashew rice**

step **2** cook the **asian orange chicken**

step **3** **serve**

luckyforyou
Fresh cut-up stir-fry vegetables are a combination of onions, bell peppers, broccoli, zucchini, carrots, and snow peas, all cut into similar-sized pieces so that they will cook at the same time.

"These tender chunks of chicken with crunchy vegetables in a flavorful garlic, ginger, and orange sauce rate well above standard take-out."

—minutemeals' Chef Sarah

step 1

prepare the **cashew rice**

- 8 cups water
- 2 bags (2-cup size) boil-in-bag rice
- 1/3 cup roasted cashews
- 1 scallion
- 1 teaspoon hot chile oil, or less to taste
- Salt and pepper to taste

1. Pour the water into a 4-quart saucepan, cover, and bring to a boil over high heat. Add the bags of rice and boil according to the directions on the package.

2. While the rice cooks, chop the cashews and scallion. Remove the bags from the water and let drain. Cut open the bags and put the rice in the saucepan. Stir in the cashews, scallion, and hot chile oil. Season with salt and pepper. Cover to keep warm.

step 2

cook the **asian orange chicken**

- 1 navel orange
- 3 tablespoons teriyaki sauce
- 1 teaspoon cornstarch
- 1 pound chicken tenders
- 2 tablespoons vegetable oil
- 5 cups cut-up fresh stir-fry vegetables
- 2 teaspoons pre-chopped garlic
- 2 teaspoons pre-minced ginger

1. Wash the orange and with a grater or lemon zester, remove the zest. Squeeze the juice. In a small bowl, stir together the orange juice, teriyaki sauce, and cornstarch.

2. Cut the chicken into 1-inch chunks.

3. In a large nonstick skillet, heat 1 tablespoon of the vegetable oil over high heat. Add the chicken and stir-fry for 1 to 2 minutes, or until no longer pink. With a slotted spoon, transfer the chicken to a plate.

4. Add the remaining 1 tablespoon of oil and the vegetables to the skillet. Reduce the heat to medium-high and stir-fry 2 to 4 minutes.

5. Add the garlic, ginger, and orange zest and stir-fry for 1 minute. Add the chicken and any juices that have accumulated on the plate and the orange juice mixture and cook, stirring constantly, until the sauce thickens slightly and the chicken is cooked through. Remove the skillet from the heat.

step 3

serve

1. Divide the rice among 4 dinner plates and top with the chicken stir-fry.

2. When ready for dessert, scoop the ice cream into 4 dessert bowls and serve.

Asian Orange Chicken
Single serving is 1/4 of total recipe
CALORIES 251; PROTEIN 25g; CARBS 15g;
TOTAL FAT 10g; SAT FAT 1g; CHOLESTEROL 63mg;
SODIUM 595mg; FIBER 3g

cranberry-sauced chicken thighs

raisin couscous

green bean salad on baby greens

brownies with vanilla frozen yogurt

menu gameplan

shopping list

Skinless boneless chicken thighs

Jellied cranberry sauce

Couscous, plain or flavored

Prewashed spring or baby greens

Green bean salad or three-bean salad (from the salad bar)

Brownies

Vanilla frozen yogurt

from your pantry

Butter

Herbes de Provence or dried thyme

Salt and pepper

Onion

Fat-free reduced-sodium chicken broth

Balsamic vinegar

Raisins, dark or golden

serves 4

beforeyoustart

Preheat the oven to 450°F to roast the chicken thighs.

step **1** make the **cranberry-sauced chicken thighs**

step **2** while the chicken bakes, prepare the **raisin couscous**

step **3** assemble the **green bean salad on baby greens**

step **4** **serve**

luckyforyou Skinned and boned chicken thighs are available in packages in most supermarkets. If you can't find large ones, use 8 smaller ones and adjust the bake time down to about 6 to 8 minutes.

"Because of the cranberry sauce, you might expect the chicken to be on the sweet side, but it's actually rich and savory." —minutemeals' Chef Ruth

step 1

make the **cranberry-sauced chicken thighs**

3 tablespoons butter

4 large (roaster-size) skinless boneless chicken thighs (1⅓ to 1½ pounds total weight)

1 teaspoon herbes de Provence or dried thyme

Salt and pepper to taste

1 medium onion

1 can (8 ounces) jellied cranberry sauce

1 cup fat-free reduced-sodium chicken broth

1 to 2 tablespoons balsamic vinegar

1. Preheat the oven to 450°F.

2. Melt 1 tablespoon of the butter in a heavy medium ovenproof skillet over medium heat. Season the chicken thighs with ½ teaspoon of the herbes de Provence and salt and pepper. Place the thighs in the skillet and lightly brown on both sides, about 3 minutes.

3. Transfer the skillet to the oven. Bake the thighs for 10 minutes, or until cooked through and the juices run clear, or until a meat thermometer inserted into thickest part registers 160° to 165°F.

4. While the chicken is baking, chop the onion.

5. Melt the remaining 2 tablespoons butter in a medium skillet. Add the onion and remaining ½ teaspoon herbes de Provence and cook, stirring, until the onion is slightly softened, about 2 minutes.

6. With a fork, partially break up the cranberry sauce. Add the cranberry sauce, chicken broth, and 1 to 2 tablespoons balsamic vinegar to the skillet. Cover and bring to a boil, then reduce the heat to low, and simmer, stirring, until partially reduced, about 5 minutes.

step 2

prepare the **raisin couscous**

1 box plain or flavored couscous (enough for 4 servings)

¼ cup dark or golden raisins

Prepare the couscous according to the directions on the package. If using unflavored couscous, season with salt and pepper. When the water is fully absorbed, fluff with a fork and stir in the raisins. Cover to keep warm.

step 3

assemble the **green bean salad on baby greens**

1 bag (5 ounces) prewashed spring or baby greens

8 ounces green bean salad or three-bean salad

Divide the salad greens among 4 salad bowls. Spoon green bean salad over them. Place the bowls on the table.

step 4

serve

1. Transfer the chicken thighs to a serving platter and cover loosely to keep warm.

2. Add the cranberry sauce mixture to the skillet used to cook the chicken, and stir to incorporate the juices and browned bits. Season with salt and pepper. Pour the cranberry sauce over the chicken. Place the platter on the table.

3. Spoon the couscous into a bowl and serve.

4. When ready for dessert, place a brownie on each of 4 dessert plates, top with a scoop of vanilla frozen yogurt, and serve.

Cranberry-Sauced Chicken Thighs
Single serving is ¼ of total recipe

CALORIES 408; PROTEIN 30g; CARBS 24g; TOTAL FAT 21g; SAT FAT 9g; CHOLESTEROL 131mg; SODIUM 420mg; FIBER 1g

barbecued chicken thighs

corn bread stuffing

mixed vegetables with lemon-sage butter

applesauce and oatmeal raisin cookies

menu gameplan

shopping list

Chili sauce

Skinless boneless chicken thighs

Corn bread stuffing mix

Frozen mixed vegetables

Lemon (for juice)

Applesauce (16-ounce jar)

Oatmeal raisin cookies

from your pantry

Nonstick vegetable cooking spray

Maple syrup

Grainy mustard

Cider vinegar

Vegetable oil

Dried red pepper flakes

Salt and pepper

Butter

Dried sage

serves 4

beforeyoustart

Preheat the broiler.

step	1	make the **barbecued chicken thighs**
step	2	prepare the **corn bread stuffing**
step	3	cook the **mixed vegetables with lemon-sage butter**
step	4	**serve**

luckyforyou You make the barbecue sauce here. You'll need 1 bowl, and a total of only 6 ingredients.

"This is a 'down-homey' menu that will please grandpa as well as the kids. It also happens to 'double' beautifully."

—minutemeals' Chef Ruth

step 1

make the **barbecued chicken thighs**

Nonstick vegetable cooking spray

2/3 cup store-bought chili sauce

1/2 cup maple syrup

2 tablespoons grainy mustard

2 tablespoons cider vinegar

2 tablespoons vegetable oil

1/4 teaspoon dried red pepper flakes

8 small skinless boneless chicken thighs (about 1 1/2 pounds total weight)

Salt and pepper to taste

1. Preheat the broiler. Line the broiler pan with aluminum foil. Coat the broiler-pan rack with nonstick vegetable cooking spray.

2. In a bowl, stir together the chili sauce, maple syrup, mustard, vinegar, vegetable oil, and pepper flakes.

3. Season the chicken thighs with salt and pepper. Dip the chicken thighs in the barbecue sauce, coating them completely. Place on the prepared broiler-rack pan. Broil the chicken, 5 to 6 inches from the heat, until tender and juicy but cooked through, about 12 minutes. Turn the thighs several times during

broiling and brush with remaining sauce. (Don't use any remaining sauce as a table sauce and don't brush it on the chicken during the last minute of cooking.)

step 2

prepare the **corn bread stuffing**

1 package (6 ounces) corn bread stuffing mix

Butter as needed

In a medium saucepan, prepare the stuffing mix according to the directions on the package. Keep warm, covered.

step 3

cook the **mixed vegetables with lemon-sage butter**

1 bag (16 ounces) frozen mixed vegetables

1/4 cup water

2 tablespoons butter

1 tablespoon fresh lemon juice (1/2 large lemon)

1/2 teaspoon crumbled dried sage

Salt and pepper to taste

1. Put the vegetables and water in a large deep skillet. Cover and bring to a boil over high heat.

Reduce the heat to medium and cook, stirring often, until the vegetables are heated though and tender, about 5 minutes. Drain and transfer to a serving dish.

2. Add the butter to the skillet and melt over medium heat. Stir in the lemon juice and sage and let bubble for 1 minute. Pour over the vegetables. Season with salt and pepper.

step 4

serve

1. Place the chicken on a serving platter.

2. Fluff the stuffing with a fork and transfer to a serving bowl. Place on the table.

3. Place the mixed vegetables on the table.

4. When ready for dessert, serve the applesauce in 4 dessert bowls, with the oatmeal cookies as an accompaniment or crumbled over the top.

Barbecued Chicken Thighs
Single serving is 1/4 of total recipe
CALORIES 488; PROTEIN 34g; CARBS 39g; TOTAL FAT 21g; SAT FAT 4g; CHOLESTEROL 121mg; SODIUM 907mg; FIBER 1g

☆ hot chicken and bacon salad

tomato juice refreshers
crusty garlic bread
sliced strawberries
with berry yogurt

shopping list

Frozen garlic bread

Strawberries

Mixed berry yogurt

Prewashed baby spinach leaves

Bacon

Italian salad dressing

Skinless boneless chicken thighs

Chives, fresh, frozen or dried

Tomato juice
(32-ounce bottle)

from the salad bar

Peeled hard-cooked eggs

Mushroom slices
(or from the produce department)

from your pantry

Dijon mustard

Salt and pepper

menu
gameplan

serves 4

beforeyoustart

Preheat the oven according to package directions to heat the garlic bread.

step 1 heat the **crusty garlic bread**

step 2 prepare the **sliced strawberries with berry yogurt**

step 3 make the **hot chicken and bacon salad**

step 4 **serve**

headsup
The chicken will be easier to cut into even strips if you chill it in the freezer for about 30 minutes.

"This salad is a new version of the old favorite, wilted spinach salad. Vary it further with crumbled blue cheese or small pitted ripe olives."

—minutemeals' Chef Ruth

step 1

heat the **crusty garlic bread**

1 loaf frozen garlic bread

Preheat the oven and warm the garlic bread according to the directions on the package. Slice the bread, place in a napkin-lined basket, and cover to keep warm.

step 2

prepare the **sliced strawberries with berry yogurt**

1 pint fresh strawberries (or 4 servings sliced strawberries from the salad bar)

1 container (8 ounces) mixed berry yogurt

Wash, hull, and slice the strawberries. Place the berries in 4 dessert dishes. Top each serving with a few tablespoons of the mixed berry yogurt. Chill until serving time.

step 3

make the **hot chicken and bacon salad**

1 bag (10 ounces) prewashed baby spinach leaves

4 slices bacon

$1/2$ cup Italian salad dressing

$1/2$ teaspoon Dijon mustard

4 peeled hard-cooked eggs

3 small or 2 large skinless boneless chicken thighs (about $3/4$ pound)

Salt and pepper to taste

$1 1/2$ cups mushroom slices

3 tablespoons chopped fresh, frozen, or dried chives

1. Place the spinach in a large salad bowl.

2. Cut the bacon crosswise into 1-inch pieces. Cook and stir bacon in a large nonstick skillet or wok over medium heat until crisp, about 4 minutes. With a slotted spoon, transfer bacon to paper towels to drain.

3. While bacon is cooking, in a measuring cup, stir together the salad dressing and mustard. Cut the eggs into quarters. Cut the chicken thighs into $1/2$-inch-thick strips, trimming off any fat. Season with salt and pepper.

4. Remove all but about 1 tablespoon bacon drippings from the skillet. Add the mushrooms to the skillet. Stir-fry for about 2 minutes, or until hot and lightly browned on the edges.

5. Add the chicken to the skillet and stir-fry for about 3 minutes, or until cooked through. Add the chives and the reserved dressing mixture. Heat until very hot. Pour the hot chicken and mushroom mixture over the spinach and toss to blend. Top with the quartered eggs and bacon.

step 4

serve

1. Pour the tomato juice into 4 tall glasses and place on the table.

2. Place the salad bowl on the table with 4 dinner plates. Serve with the warm garlic bread.

3. When ready for dessert, serve the yogurt-topped strawberries.

Hot Chicken and Bacon Salad
Single serving is $1/4$ of total recipe
CALORIES 434; PROTEIN 28g; CARBS 7g;
TOTAL FAT 33g; SAT FAT 8g; CHOLESTEROL 281mg;
SODIUM 714mg; FIBER 2g

turkey saltimbocca

balsamic-basil tomatoes
buttered peas
crusty seeded breadsticks
lemon berry cheesecakes

menu gameplan

serves 4

shopping list

Ripe tomatoes

Fresh basil

Frozen baby peas

Turkey cutlets

Sliced prosciutto
(from the deli counter) or
thinly sliced baked ham

Thin slices of mozzarella
(from the deli counter)

Crusty seeded breadsticks

Frozen individual plain
cheesecakes (4)

Jarred lemon curd (1/2 cup)

Fresh raspberries or blueberries
(1/2 cup)

from your pantry

Balsamic vinegar

Extra virgin olive oil

Salt and pepper

Butter

Ground dried sage

Dry white wine

step	1	assemble the **balsamic-basil tomatoes**
step	2	cook the **buttered peas**
step	3	cook the **turkey saltimbocca**
step	4	**serve**

headsup Turkey cutlets, depending on the brand, will vary in thickness, anywhere from 1/4 to 3/8 inch thick. They cook quickly: Cut into the edge of the cutlet to check for doneness. The cutlet should be opaque—no longer pink inside.

"Veal saltimbocca is a favorite on Italian restaurant menus. Make it at home, with turkey, for a fraction of the cost."

—minutemeals' Chef Sarah

step 1

assemble the **balsamic-basil tomatoes**

3 ripe medium tomatoes

1/3 cup fresh basil leaves

1 tablespoon balsamic vinegar

1 tablespoon extra virgin olive oil

Salt and pepper to taste

Slice the tomatoes and arrange on a serving platter. Stack the basil leaves, cut into thin slivers with scissors, and scatter them over the tomatoes. Drizzle with the vinegar and olive oil and season with salt and pepper. Place the platter on the table.

step 2

cook the **buttered peas**

1 package (10 ounces) frozen baby peas

1 tablespoon butter

In a medium saucepan, cook the baby peas according to the directions on the package. Drain, add the butter, and cover until serving time.

step 3

cook the **turkey saltimbocca**

3 tablespoons butter

4 turkey cutlets (about 1 pound)

1 teaspoon ground dried sage

Salt and pepper to taste

4 thin slices prosciutto or thinly sliced baked ham

4 thin slices mozzarella cheese

1/2 cup dry white wine

1. In a large (12-inch) heavy non-stick skillet, melt 2 tablespoons of the butter over medium-high heat.

2. While the butter heats, sprinkle the turkey cutlets with sage and salt and pepper on both sides. When butter is sizzling, add the cutlets to the skillet. Cook for 1 minute, until browned on the underside. Turn the cutlets. Top with the proscuitto, folding it in half to fit, and the mozzarella cheese. Cover the skillet and cook for 1 minute, or until the cutlets are cooked through, opaque, and the cheese is melted. Remove the skillet from heat; transfer the cutlets to a serving platter, and cover loosely with foil.

3. Return the skillet to the heat and add the wine. Cook, stirring constantly and scraping up the brown bits on the bottom of the pan, for 1 to 2 minutes, or until the wine is reduced by about half. Remove the skillet from the heat, add the remaining 1 tablespoon butter, and swirl just until melted. Season with salt and pepper. Spoon the sauce over the cutlets.

step 4

serve

1. Place the turkey saltimbocca on the table with the tomato salad. Serve on 4 dinner plates.

2. Toss the peas, transfer them to a serving bowl, and place the bowl on the table.

3. Serve the breadsticks in a basket.

4. When ready for dessert, place a cheesecake on each of 4 dessert plates. Spoon lemon curd over the top of each and sprinkle with fresh berries. Serve.

Turkey Saltimbocca
Single serving is 1/4 of total recipe

CALORIES 269; PROTEIN 34g; CARBS 1g; TOTAL FAT 14g; SAT FAT 8g; CHOLESTEROL 121mg; SODIUM 423mg; FIBER 0g

sautéed turkey
with peaches and basil
zucchini with mint
bittersweet brownie mousse

menu
gameplan

shopping list

Chocolate chips

Heavy cream

Brownies

Fresh mint

Zucchini

Lemon (for juice)

Fresh basil

Peaches

Turkey cutlets

from your pantry

Coffee liqueur
(or brewed coffee)

Butter

Salt and pepper

All-purpose flour

Dry red wine

serves 4

beforeyoustart

Refrigerate the bowl and beaters to make the mousse.

| step | 1 | make the **bittersweet brownie mousse** |

| step | 2 | cook the **zucchini with mint** |

| step | 3 | make the **sautéed turkey** |

| step | 4 | **serve** |

headsup
Fresh herbs add great flavor and they are available year round. For optimum flavor, add delicate herbs like basil and mint at the last minute.

"This menu is definitely special enough for company. It tastes as if it took hours to prepare."

—minutemeals' Chef Sarah

step 1

make the **bittersweet brownie mousse**

1/2 cup bittersweet or semisweet chocolate chips

1/2 cup heavy cream, chilled

1 tablespoon coffee liqueur or brewed coffee

4 brownies

1. In a small microwave-safe bowl, place the chocolate chips and 1 tablespoon of the cream. Microwave on High for 1 minute. Stir until the chips are melted. Let cool for a few minutes. Stir in the liqueur or coffee.

2. In chilled bowl, whip the remaining cream to stiff peaks with an electric mixer. Spoon the chocolate mixture over the whipped cream. Fold it into cream until no streaks of white remain.

3. Cut the brownies into bite-sized pieces and place in 4 dessert dishes. Spoon mousse over the brownies and refrigerate until serving.

step 2

cook the **zucchini with mint**

2 tablespoons chopped fresh mint

2 medium zucchini

1 tablespoon butter

Salt and pepper to taste

Fresh lemon juice to taste

1. Chop enough mint to measure 2 tablespoons. Trim and slice the zucchini.

2. In a medium microwave-safe bowl, place the zucchini, butter, and salt and pepper. Cover with the lid or vented plastic wrap. Microwave on High for 2 minutes. Stir, cover, and microwave for 2 to 3 minutes longer, or until the zucchini is tender. Keep warm, covered.

step 3

make the **sautéed turkey with peaches and basil**

1/2 cup fresh basil leaves

2 firm-ripe peaches or nectarines (or use 4 to 6 plums)

3 tablespoons butter

4 turkey cutlets (about 1 pound)

Salt and pepper to taste

2 tablespoons all-purpose flour

1/2 cup dry red wine

1. Rinse the basil leaves, pat dry, and stack. Cut into thin strips with scissors. Slice and pit the peaches.

2. In a large (12-inch) heavy non-stick skillet, melt the butter over medium-high heat. While the butter melts, season the turkey slices with salt and pepper on both sides. Dust with the flour.

3. When the butter is sizzling, add the turkey cutlets in one layer to the skillet. Cook for 2 minutes per side, until browned and no longer pink in the thickest part. Transfer the cutlets to a serving platter and keep warm, loosely covered.

4. Add the wine to the skillet and stir to scrape up any brown bits on the bottom. Add the peaches and cook, stirring frequently, for 2 minutes, until the wine is reduced slightly. Stir in the slivered basil and season with salt and pepper. Remove the skillet from the heat and spoon the sauce over the turkey.

step 4

serve

1. Divide the turkey cutlets with peaches and basil evenly among 4 dinner plates.

2. Add the mint and lemon juice to taste to the zucchini, toss to combine, and divide the zucchini evenly among the 4 dinner plates. Serve.

3. When ready for dessert, serve the mousse.

Sautéed Turkey with Peaches and Basil
Single serving is 1/4 of total recipe

CALORIES 245; PROTEIN 31g; CARBS 8g; TOTAL FAT 10g; SAT FAT 6g; CHOLESTEROL 105mg; SODIUM 198mg; FIBER 1g

potato, turkey, and green bean salad
with warm bacon dressing

grape tomatoes

crusty rolls or crackers

cherry fruit Popsicles

menu gameplan

serves 4

step	1	make the **potato, turkey, and green bean salad**
step	2	plate the **grape tomatoes**
step	3	**serve**

shopping list

New potatoes

Frozen cut green beans

Bacon

Sweet white onion

Thin-sliced turkey breast (from the deli counter)

Prewashed mixed baby or spring greens

Grape tomatoes

Crusty rolls or crackers

Cherry fruit Popsicles

from your pantry

Salt

Cider vinegar

Sugar

Dijon mustard

Dill pickle

Olive oil

Freshly ground black pepper

luckyforyou Some supermarkets carry precut precooked potatoes in bags in the produce department. They can be used, with no further cooking needed, in this salad.

"There's something about a warm dressing that makes a salad special. This one is no different. Assemble and enjoy!"

—minutemeals' Chef Sarah

step 1

make the **potato, turkey, and green bean salad with warm bacon dressing**

1¼ pounds small new potatoes

Salt to taste

1½ cups frozen cut green beans

5 slices bacon

¼ cup cider vinegar

1½ tablespoons sugar

1 tablespoon Dijon mustard

½ large sweet white onion

¾ pound thin-sliced turkey breast

1 medium dill pickle

1 tablespoon olive oil

Freshly ground black pepper to taste

1 bag (5 ounces) prewashed mixed baby or spring greens

1. Cut the potatoes into 1-inch chunks. Put them in a large saucepan and add 1 inch cold water and salt to taste. Cover and bring to a boil over high heat. Reduce the heat to medium, and cook, partially covered, for 5 minutes. Stir in the green beans and cook for 2 min-

utes longer, or until the beans are hot and the potatoes are fork-tender. Drain and return to the pan. Cover to keep warm.

2. Meanwhile, in a large nonstick skillet, fry the bacon over medium-high heat until crisp, about 4 minutes. Drain on paper towels. Discard all but 3 tablespoons fat from the skillet.

3. In a cup, with a fork, mix the vinegar, sugar, and mustard until blended.

4. Thinly slice the onion. Cut the turkey breast into 1-inch pieces. Coarsely chop the pickle.

5. Add the onion to the bacon fat in the skillet and cook, stirring often, until nearly tender, about 1 minute. Pour in the vinegar mixture, cover, and bring to a boil, stirring. Scrape into a large salad bowl.

6. In the same skillet, warm the olive oil over high heat. Add the turkey, season with salt and pepper, and cook, stirring often, until lightly browned and no longer pink inside when tested. Add to the onion mixture in the bowl.

7. Add the potatoes and beans, baby greens, and chopped pickle to the bowl. Toss well and season with salt and pepper (remember that you'll be adding the bacon). Crumble the bacon on top.

step 2

plate the **grape tomatoes**

1 pint grape tomatoes

Rinse the tomatoes, shake dry, and place in a shallow serving bowl. Place the bowl on the table.

step 3

serve

1. Place the salad bowl on the table. Serve the salad on 4 dinner plates with the rolls or crackers and tomatoes as accompaniments.

2. When ready for dessert, serve the Popsicles directly from the freezer.

Potato, Turkey, and Green Bean Salad
Single serving is ¼ of total recipe

CALORIES 384; PROTEIN 24g; CARBS 35g; TOTAL FAT 18g; SAT FAT 5g; CHOLESTEROL 48mg; SODIUM 1,676mg; FIBER 6g

turkey reuben sandwiches
potato salad
cherry tomatoes
red and green grapes

menu gameplan

serves 4

beforeyoustart
Rinse the grapes in a colander and let stand until serving time.

step 1 plate the **potato salad** and **cherry tomatoes**

step 2 make the **turkey reuben sandwiches**

step 3 **serve**

---

shopping list
Prepared potato salad (from the deli counter)

Thousand Island dressing

Smoked or roast turkey, thin-sliced (from the deli counter)

Prepared sauerkraut

Swiss cheese, sliced

from the salad bar
Cherry tomatoes

Red and green grapes (or from the produce department)

from your pantry
Butter

Rye bread

Dill pickle spears

---

luckyforyou Store-bought dressings are a great convenience. If you don't happen to have Thousand Island on hand, though, make your own: Mix together 3 tablespoons mayonnaise, 1 tablespoon chili sauce or ketchup, and 2 teaspoons drained pickle relish.

"Trust me, you won't miss the corned beef in these 'healthier' Reubens, which, incidentally, can be assembled a full hour in advance of cooking."

—minutemeals' Chef Paul

step 1

plate the **potato salad and cherry tomatoes**

Prepared potato salad for 4

1 pint cherry tomatoes

1. Place the potato salad on a serving plate.

2. Rinse the cherry tomatoes, shake dry, and transfer to a serving plate. Place the plates on the table.

step 2

make the **turkey reuben sandwiches**

2 tablespoons softened butter

8 slices rye bread

1/4 cup store-bought Thousand Island dressing

3/4 pound thin-sliced smoked or roast turkey

3/4 cup drained prepared sauerkraut

4 slices Swiss cheese (about 3 ounces)

Dill pickle spears for serving

1. Spread butter on one side of each slice of bread. Place them, buttered side down, on a sheet of waxed paper. Spread Thousand Island dressing on all the bread slices.

2. Arrange turkey on 4 of the slices, dividing it evenly. Spoon sauerkraut onto the turkey, dividing it evenly and spreading in an even thickness. Place Swiss cheese on top of the sauerkraut. Top with the remaining 4 slices of bread, buttered side up.

3. Place a nonstick skillet (or a grill pan or large griddle) over medium heat. Add 2 sandwiches and cook for 2 minutes. Turn and cook for 2 minutes, until golden. With a spatula, transfer the sandwiches to a cutting board and keep warm, loosely covered. Cook the remaining 2 sandwiches in the same way.

step 3

serve

1. Cut each sandwich in half on the diagonal and place on a plate. Garnish with a dill pickle spear. Serve, with the potato salad and cherry tomatoes as accompaniments.

2. When ready for dessert, place the grapes in a bowl and serve them from the bowl.

Turkey Reuben Sandwiches
Single serving is 1/4 of total recipe

CALORIES 419; PROTEIN 26g; CARBS 33g;
TOTAL FAT 20g; SAT FAT 9g; CHOLESTEROL 75mg;
SODIUM 1498mg; FIBER 4g

turkey stroganoff

glazed green beans agrodolce

cloverleaf rolls

chunky cherry and chocolate frozen yogurt

serves 4

---

shopping list

Wide egg noodles

Mushroom slices
(from the salad bar or produce department)

Thick-sliced roast turkey breast (from the deli counter)

Scallions

Reduced-fat or regular sour cream

Pretrimmed green beans

Cloverleaf rolls

Chunky cherry and chocolate frozen yogurt

from your pantry

Salt and pepper

Fat-free reduced-sodium chicken broth

All-purpose flour

Poultry seasoning

Butter

White balsamic or red wine vinegar

Brown sugar

beforeyoustart

Bring a large pot of salted water to a boil, covered, over high heat to cook the noodles.

step	1	make the **turkey stroganoff**
step	2	cook the **glazed green beans agrodolce**
step	3	**serve**

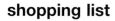

headsup   Be sure to incorporate the sour cream as directed in the Stroganoff recipe. If you try to save time by adding the sour cream to the skillet, you run the risk of it curdling and ruining the sauce.

"Stroganoff is a good dish for entertaining. And when made with turkey and reduced-fat sour cream, like this one, it becomes even more appealing."

—minutemeals' Chef Paul

step 1
make the **turkey stroganoff**

Salt to taste

12 ounces wide egg noodles (about 6 cups)

1 can (14 1/2 ounces) fat-free reduced-sodium chicken broth

2 tablespoons all-purpose flour

1 package (8 ounces) mushroom slices

1 teaspoon poultry seasoning

8 ounces thick-sliced roast turkey breast (1/4 inch thick)

4 scallions

1 cup reduced-fat or regular sour cream

1. Pour water into a large pot, salt lightly, and cover. Bring to a boil over high heat. Add the egg noodles and cook according to the directions on the package until just tender. Remove 1/2 cup of the cooking water, then drain well in a colander. Return the noodles to the pot and cover to keep warm.

2. Meanwhile, whisk together the chicken broth and flour in a large (12- to 14-inch) nonstick skillet until blended. Add the mushrooms and poultry seasoning. Cover and bring to boil over medium-high heat, stirring occasionally. Uncover and simmer for 5 minutes, stirring often, until lightly thickened.

3. While the sauce simmers, cut the turkey into 1/4-inch-wide strips; slice the scallions.

4. Stir the turkey and scallions into the skillet, remove it from the heat, and cover to keep warm.

step 2
cook the **glazed green beans agrodolce**

1 pound pretrimmed fresh green beans

2 tablespoons butter

2 tablespoons white balsamic or red wine vinegar

1 tablespoon brown sugar

Salt and pepper to taste

1. Bring 1/2 inch water to a boil, covered, in a large skillet over high heat. Add the beans to the pan, cover, and cook over medium heat for 4 to 6 minutes, or just until tender. Drain well.

2. Put the butter, vinegar, and sugar in the skillet. Add the hot cooked beans and toss until coated and the butter is melted. Season with salt and pepper. Transfer to a serving bowl and cover loosely to keep warm.

step 3
serve

1. Finish the Stroganoff: Put the sour cream in a bowl. Stir in a little of the hot sauce from the skillet, then stir the mixture into the skillet until combined.

2. Pour the turkey Stroganoff over the egg noodles and stir to combine. If the mixture is thick, add a little of the reserved noodle cooking water. Transfer the Stroganoff to a serving bowl or serve from the skillet.

3. Place the green beans on the table with the cloverleaf rolls.

4. When ready for dessert, scoop the frozen yogurt into 4 dessert bowls and serve.

Turkey Stroganoff
Single serving is 1/4 of total recipe (analyzed using reduced-fat sour cream)
CALORIES 459; PROTEIN 24g; CARBS 64g; TOTAL FAT 12g; SAT FAT 6g; CHOLESTEROL 122mg; SODIUM 1300mg; FIBER 5g

turkey and orzo salad
with tomatoes and corn
whole-grain flatbreads
strawberry gelato, whole strawberries, and pirouette cookies

shopping list

Orzo

Frozen corn kernels

Thick-sliced roast turkey breast (from the deli counter)

Provolone cheese, sliced

Prepared pesto

Lemon (for juice)

Pre-chopped pecans or walnuts

Tomatoes

Prewashed baby spinach leaves

Whole-grain flatbreads

Strawberries

Strawberry gelato

Pirouette cookies

from your pantry

Salt and pepper

Mayonnaise, regular or reduced-fat

serves 4

beforeyoustart

Bring a pot of water to a boil, covered, over high heat to cook the orzo.

step **1** make the **turkey and orzo salad with tomatoes and corn**

step **2** heat the **whole-grain flatbreads**

step **3** prepare the **dessert**

step **4** **serve**

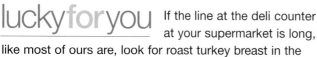

luckyforyou If the line at the deli counter at your supermarket is long, like most of ours are, look for roast turkey breast in the prepared foods section, where you may find a piece individually packaged.

"This spin on pasta salad, with pesto and provolone, is great-looking and wonderful in summer with locally grown tomatoes."

—minutemeals' Chef Paul

step 1

make the turkey and orzo salad with tomatoes and corn

2 quarts water

Salt to taste

1¹/₂ cups orzo

1¹/₂ cups frozen corn kernels

8 ounces thick-sliced roast turkey breast, cut ¹/₄ inch thick

4 ounces sliced provolone cheese

¹/₄ cup regular or reduced-fat mayonnaise

3 tablespoons prepared pesto

1¹/₂ tablespoons fresh lemon juice (1 lemon)

¹/₄ cup pre-chopped pecans or walnuts

Pepper to taste

3 ripe medium tomatoes

4 cups prewashed baby spinach leaves

1. Pour the water into a large saucepan, salt lightly, and cover. Bring to a boil over high heat. Add the orzo and return to a boil, stirring often. Cook, stirring occasionally, for 8 minutes. Stir in the corn and cook 2 to 3 minutes, or until the corn and orzo are tender. Drain in a colander and rinse briefly under cold running water. Drain again.

2. Remove the skin, if any, on the turkey breast and cut the meat into ¹/₄-inch cubes. Cut the provolone into strips.

3. In a large bowl, with a fork, mix the mayonnaise, pesto, and lemon juice until blended. Add the orzo and corn mixture, the turkey, provolone, nuts, and salt and pepper to taste. Toss well.

4. Cut the tomatoes into wedges.

5. Mound the spinach leaves on a large platter. Spoon the salad in the center and surround with the tomato wedges. Place the bowl on the table.

step 2

heat the whole-grain flatbreads

4 to 6 whole-grain flatbreads

Stack the flatbreads, wrap the stack loosely in aluminum foil, and place in a toaster oven until warmed through. Transfer the breads to a napkin-lined basket, cover to keep warm, and place the basket on the table.

step 3

prepare the strawberry gelato, whole strawberries, and pirouette cookies

¹/₂ pint ripe strawberries

1 pint strawberry gelato

1 box pirouette cookies or other rolled wafer cookies

1. Rinse the strawberries and remove the hulls.

2. Remove the gelato from the freezer to soften slightly, if desired.

3. Place the cookies on a serving plate.

step 4

serve

1. Serve the turkey salad on 4 dinner plates, accompanied by the flatbreads.

2. When ready for dessert, scoop the gelato into 4 dessert bowls, garnish each serving with whole strawberries and serve. Pass the pirouettes at the table.

Turkey and Orzo Salad with Tomatoes and Corn
Single serving is ¹/₄ of total recipe
CALORIES 681; PROTEIN 32g; CARBS 71g; TOTAL FAT 32g; SAT FAT 9g; CHOLESTEROL 53mg; SODIUM 1232mg; FIBER 6g

turkey picadillo
green salad olé
flan and wafer cookies

menu
gameplan

serves 4

shopping list

Green pepper

Dark raisins

Lean ground turkey

Diced tomatoes, Italian-style

Reduced-fat sour cream

Chopped scallions
(from the salad bar)

Prewashed colorful crisp
salad greens

Pre-shredded Cheddar
cheese

Pimiento-stuffed salad olives

Individual flans

Wafer cookies

from your pantry

Onion

Garlic

Olive oil

Chili powder

Salt and pepper

Vinaigrette dressing,
store-bought

step **1** cook the **turkey picadillo**

step **2** assemble the **green salad olé**

step **3** plate the **flan**

step **4** **serve**

lucky**foryou** Picadillo can also be used
as a hearty pasta sauce or
as a filling for tortillas.

"A nice blend of traditional ingredients plus an unusually pretty presentation turn this non-beef version of picadillo into a super party dish."

—minutemeals' Chef Hillary

step 1

cook the **turkey picadillo**

- 1 medium green pepper
- 1 small onion
- 2 garlic cloves
- 1 tablespoon olive oil
- 2 teaspoons chili powder
- 1/2 cup dark raisins
- 1 pound lean ground turkey
- 1 can (15 ounces) Italian-style diced tomatoes
- Salt and pepper to taste
- 1/3 cup reduced-fat sour cream for serving
- 4 tablespoons chopped scallions for serving

1. Coarsely chop the green pepper and onion. Crush the garlic cloves in a garlic press.

2. Heat the olive oil in a large cast-iron skillet over high heat. Add the pepper, onion, garlic, and chili powder and cook, stirring often, for 3 minutes, or until the vegetables are nearly tender. Stir in the raisins and cook for 1 minute.

3. Add the turkey, breaking it up with a fork, and cook for 5 minutes, or until no longer pink. Stir in the diced tomatoes, undrained, and bring to a boil, covered. Reduce the heat to medium-low and simmer for 2 to 3 minutes, or until slightly thickened. Season with salt and pepper.

step 2

assemble the **green salad olé**

- 6 cups prewashed colorful crisp salad greens
- 1 cup pre-shredded Cheddar cheese
- 1/3 cup pimiento-stuffed salad olives
- 2 to 4 tablespoons store-bought vinaigrette dressing

In a large bowl, toss the salad greens with the Cheddar, olives, and vinaigrette.

step 3

plate the **flan**

- 4 individual store-bought flans
- Wafer cookies

Place 1 flan on each of 4 dessert plates.

step 4

serve

1. Mound the picadillo in the center of a large platter with sides.

2. Arrange the salad around the picadillo on the platter. Spoon the sour cream over the picadillo and sprinkle with the scallions. Serve.

3. When ready for dessert, garnish each flan with a wafer cookie and serve.

Turkey Picadillo
Single serving is 1/4 of total recipe
CALORIES 307; PROTEIN 18g; CARBS 31g; TOTAL FAT 13g; SAT FAT 4g; CHOLESTEROL 77mg; SODIUM 667mg; FIBER 3g

turkey soong

miso soup
asian cucumber salad
lemon and lime sorbet coupes

shopping list

Gingerroot

Water chestnuts

Chopped scallions
(from the salad bar)

Lean ground turkey

Prewashed iceberg or leaf
lettuce leaves

Instant miso soup

Carrot

English cucumber

Lemon sorbet

Lime sorbet

from your pantry

Vegetable oil

Dry sherry

Teriyaki sauce

Cornstarch

Rice vinegar

Lite soy sauce

Toasted sesame oil

Sugar

serves 4

step	1	cook the **turkey soong**
step	2	make the **miso soup**
step	3	prepare the **asian cucumber salad**
step	4	**serve**

 Turkey Soong can be served warm or at room temperature.

"Add Chinese chili paste, with or without garlic, and cilantro to the turkey Soong, if you like. It's how it's served, though, that makes it fun."

—minutemeals' Chef Hillary

step 1

cook the **turkey soong**

2-inch piece fresh gingerroot

1 can (5 ounces) water chestnuts

1 tablespoon vegetable oil

1½ cups chopped scallions

1 pound lean ground turkey

¾ cup dry sherry

¼ cup teriyaki sauce

1 tablespoon cornstarch

Prewashed large iceberg or leaf lettuce leaves

1. Peel and coarsely chop the ginger. Drain and coarsely chop the water chestnuts.

2. Heat the vegetable oil in a large, deep, heavy skillet over high heat. Stir in the ginger and scallions and cook, stirring, for 1 to 2 minutes, until the scallions are tender. Add the turkey and cook, breaking it up with a fork, about 5 minutes, until browned. Stir in the water chestnuts.

3. In a small bowl, stir together the sherry, teriyaki sauce, and cornstarch until the cornstarch is dissolved. Add to the turkey mixture, cover and bring to a boil, stirring. Boil for 1 minute, until slightly thickened. Remove the pan from the heat.

step 2

make the **miso soup**

Instant miso soup (for 4 servings)

1 medium carrot

1. Prepare the soup according to the directions on the package. Keep warm, covered.

2. While the soup cools, peel and grate 1 medium carrot for garnish.

step 3

prepare the **asian cucumber salad**

1 large English cucumber

1 tablespoon vegetable oil

2 teaspoons rice vinegar

2 teaspoons lite soy sauce

1 teaspoon toasted sesame oil

¼ teaspoon sugar

1. Thinly slice the cucumber. Place the slices in a medium bowl.

2. In a cup, stir together the vegetable oil, vinegar, soy sauce, sesame oil, and sugar. Pour the dressing over the cucumber slices, toss to coat, and place the bowl on the table.

step 4

serve

1. Ladle the miso soup into small bowls, scatter grated or shredded carrot on top, and serve as a first course or with the turkey Soong.

2. Transfer the turkey Soong to a shallow bowl and place the lettuce leaves on a platter. To serve, spoon some of the turkey Soong onto the center of each lettuce leaf, fold part of the leaf over to cover it, then roll into a cylinder.

3. When ready for dessert, place a scoop of lemon and lime sorbet in each of 4 dessert bowls or coupe glasses and serve.

Turkey Soong
Single serving is ¼ of total recipe
CALORIES 214; PROTEIN 17g; CARBS 12g; TOTAL FAT 11g; SAT FAT 2g; CHOLESTEROL 67mg; SODIUM 783mg; FIBER 3g

turkey hash

sliced tomatoes on baby spinach
buttermilk biscuits
strawberries with confectioners' sugar

menu
gameplan

shopping list

Red pepper

Prepared diced potatoes with onions (such as Simply Potatoes® brand)

Lean ground turkey

Heavy cream

Fresh parsley

Ripe tomatoes

Prewashed baby spinach leaves

Lemon (for juice)

Strawberries

Ready-to-serve buttermilk biscuits or dinner rolls

from your pantry

Garlic

Butter

All-purpose flour

Dried thyme

Poultry seasoning

Fat-free reduced-sodium chicken broth

Salt

Olive oil

Freshly ground black pepper

Confectioners' sugar

serves 4

step **1** cook the **turkey hash**

step **2** prepare the **sliced tomatoes on baby spinach**

step **3** prepare the **strawberries**

step **4** **serve**

luckyforyou By using precooked potatoes with onions, you've not only saved yourself valuable prep time, but the minutes it takes to season them, too.

"This is old-fashioned comfort food of the best kind. Top each serving of hash with a fried egg if you're hosting big eaters."

—minutemeals' Chef Hillary

step 1

cook the **turkey hash**

1 large red pepper

1 garlic clove

3 tablespoons butter

1 package (1 pound 4 ounces) prepared diced potatoes with onions, such as Simply Potatoes® brand

1 pound lean ground turkey

2 tablespoons all-purpose flour

1 teaspoon dried thyme

$1/2$ teaspoon poultry seasoning

$3/4$ cup fat-free reduced-sodium chicken broth

$1/4$ cup heavy cream

Salt and pepper to taste

$1/4$ cup chopped fresh parsley

1. Coarsely chop the red pepper. Crush the garlic clove though a garlic press.

2. Melt the butter in a large cast-iron skillet over high heat. Add the red pepper and garlic and cook, stirring, for 3 minutes, or until slightly softened. Add the potatoes and cook for 3 minutes, turning once. Add the turkey and break it up with a fork. Cover and cook, stirring every 2 minutes, until the turkey is no longer pink, about 4 minutes.

3. Stir in the flour, thyme, and poultry seasoning. Blend in the broth and heavy cream and bring to a simmer. Cover and simmer until the hash thickens and the potatoes are tender, about 5 to 7 minutes. Season with salt and pepper.

4. While the hash cooks, chop enough parsley to measure $1/4$ cup.

step 2

prepare the **sliced tomatoes on baby spinach**

4 ripe medium tomatoes

Prewashed baby spinach leaves for lining the platter

2 tablespoons olive oil

1 tablespoon fresh lemon juice

Salt and freshly ground pepper to taste

1. Rinse the tomatoes, pat them dry, and slice.

2. Line a serving platter with the spinach leaves. Arrange the tomato slices on the spinach, then drizzle with the olive oil and lemon juice. Season with salt and a generous amount of fresh pepper. Place the platter on the table.

step 3

prepare the **strawberries with confectioners' sugar**

1 pint small strawberries

$1/2$ cup confectioners' sugar

1. Rinse the strawberries and hull them. Divide the berries among 4 dessert bowls.

2. Put the confectioners' sugar in a small bowl.

step 4

serve

1. Right before serving, stir the fresh parsley into the hash. Spoon the hash onto dinner plates or serve it directly from the skillet at the table.

2. Serve the salad with the hash or on separate plates with the dinner rolls as an accompaniment.

3. When ready for dessert, serve the berries with the bowl of sugar for dipping.

Turkey Hash
Single serving is $1/4$ of total recipe
CALORIES 416; PROTEIN 20g; CARBS 36g;
TOTAL FAT 21g; SAT FAT 11g; CHOLESTEROL 111mg;
SODIUM 632mg; FIBER 5g

turkey sausage-and-stuffing skillet supper

steamed broccoli
mixed green salad
apple turnovers

menu
gameplan

serves 4

shopping list

Dried cranberries

Orange liqueur

Turkey sausage links

Celery

Stuffing mix

Prewashed spring or baby greens

Apple turnovers

Cheddar cheese (optional)

from the salad bar

Cherry tomatoes

Cucumber slices

Broccoli florets (or from the produce department)

from your pantry

Onion

Olive oil

Vinaigrette dressing, store-bought or homemade

---

step 1 make the **turkey sausage-and-stuffing skillet supper**

step 2 assemble the **mixed green salad**

step 3 cook the **steamed broccoli**

step 4 heat the **apple turnovers**

step 5 serve

luckyforyou Bread stuffing now comes in ready-to-use quantities that take the guesswork out of having to measure.

"You can use this skillet supper recipe as turkey stuffing. Remove the casings from the links or, simpler still, use bulk sausage."

—minutemeals' Chef Hillary

step 1

make the turkey sausage-and-stuffing skillet supper

1/2 cup dried cranberries

2 tablespoons orange liqueur or orange juice

12 ounces sweet or hot turkey sausage links

1 large onion

2 small celery stalks

1 tablespoon olive oil

1 1/2 cups water

1 box (6 ounces) one-step stuffing mix

1. Combine the cranberries and liqueur or juice in a small bowl.

2. Cut each sausage link in half crosswise. Coarsely chop the onion and celery stalks.

3. In a large deep heavy skillet, heat the olive oil over medium heat. Add the turkey sausage. Cover and cook, turning occasionally, for 3 minutes, or until lightly browned. Add the onion and celery. Cover and cook, stirring once or twice, 3 minutes, until slightly softened.

4. Stir in the soaked cranberries, including the liquid, and the water, cover and bring to a boil. Add the stuffing mix and stir well to combine. Cook for 2 minutes. Remove the pan from the heat, cover, and let stand for 2 minutes.

step 2

assemble the mixed green salad

1/2 cup cherry tomatoes

1 bag (5 ounces) prewashed spring or baby greens

1/2 cup cucumber slices

2 to 4 tablespoons vinaigrette dressing

1. Rinse the cherry tomatoes and shake dry.

2. In a large salad bowl, combine the greens, cucumber slices, tomatoes, and vinaigrette and toss. Place the bowl on the table.

step 3

cook the steamed broccoli

1 pound pretrimmed broccoli florets

Olive oil (optional)

1. Bring a pot with 1 inch water to a boil, covered, over medium-high heat.

2. Place the broccoli florets in a vegetable steamer basket. When the water is boiling, carefully place the broccoli in the pot, cover tightly, and steam for 5 minutes, or until crisp-tender. Transfer the florets to a serving bowl and drizzle with olive oil, if desired.

step 4

heat the apple turnovers

4 store-bought apple turnovers

Cheddar cheese (optional)

Place the turnovers in a toaster oven and heat on low until warmed through. Keep warm until serving time.

step 5

serve

1. Place the skillet on the table and divide the turkey sausage and stuffing evenly among 4 dinner plates.

2. Place the broccoli on the table.

3. Serve the salad on 4 salad plates, if desired.

4. When ready for dessert, place a turnover on each of 4 dessert plates and add a slice or two of Cheddar, if desired. Serve.

Turkey Sausage-and-Stuffing Skillet Supper
Single serving is 1/4 of total recipe
CALORIES 364; PROTEIN 18g; CARBS 47g; TOTAL FAT 12g; SAT FAT 3g; CHOLESTEROL 50mg; SODIUM 1206mg; FIBER 3g

turkey sausage gumbo

corn muffins

tangerines and shortbread cookies

menu
gameplan

shopping list

Turkey sausage links, Italian-style

Green pepper

Diced tomatoes

Frozen sliced okra

Frozen corn kernels

Corn muffins

Tangerines

Shortbread cookies

from your pantry

Onion

Garlic

Vegetable oil

Fat-free low-sodium chicken broth

Hot red pepper sauce (optional)

Salt and pepper

serves 4 generously

beforeyoustart

Preheat the oven to 450°F to heat the corn muffins. Thaw the okra.

step **1** make the **turkey sausage gumbo**

step **2** meanwhile, heat the **corn muffins**

step **3** **serve**

lucky**foryou** Okra, a major ingredient in gumbo, is a seasonal vegetable, except in the southern part of the country, where it can be found year-round. Frozen sliced okra makes a fine substitute here.

"How you make gumbo, especially in Louisiana, is a very personal matter! Try serving it over rice or barley for a heartier bowl."

—minutemeals' Chef Hillary

step 1

make the **turkey sausage gumbo**

12 ounces sweet or hot Italian-style turkey sausage links

1 large onion

1 medium green pepper

1 large garlic clove

1 tablespoon vegetable oil

2 cans (14$\frac{1}{2}$ ounces each) diced tomatoes

1 can (14$\frac{1}{2}$ ounces) fat-free low-sodium chicken broth

1 package (10 ounces) frozen sliced okra, thawed

1 package (10 ounces) frozen corn kernels

$\frac{1}{2}$ teaspoon hot red pepper sauce (optional)

Salt and pepper to taste

1. Cut the turkey sausage into 1-inch pieces. Chop the onion. Coarsely chop the green pepper. Crush the garlic clove in a garlic press.

2. In a large saucepan or Dutch oven, heat the vegetable oil over medium heat. Tilt the pan so that it coats the bottom and add the sausage. Cover and cook, turning occasionally, for 3 minutes, until lightly browned. Stir in the onion, green pepper, and garlic and toss to coat. Reduce the heat to low, cover, and cook for 3 minutes.

3. Drain the tomatoes; add them, the chicken broth, okra, and corn to the saucepan. Cover and bring to a boil over high heat. Reduce the heat to low and simmer, stirring often, for 3 to 5 minutes, or until the vegetables are tender and the gumbo has thickened slightly. Season with hot red pepper sauce, if desired, and salt and pepper.

step 2

heat the **corn muffins**

4 store-bought corn muffins

1. Preheat the oven to 450°F.

2. Sprinkle the muffins with a little water and wrap in aluminum foil. (The water will steam the corn muffins, heating them more quickly without drying them out.) Place in the oven for 3 to 5 minutes, or until heated through.

step 3

serve

1. Ladle the gumbo into 4 large soup bowls and serve.

2. Place the corn muffins in a napkin-lined basket and serve at once.

3. When ready for dessert, serve the tangerines from a bowl, with the shortbread cookies as an accompaniment.

Turkey Sausage Gumbo
Single serving is $\frac{1}{4}$ of total recipe
CALORIES 287; PROTEIN 18g; CARBS 35g; TOTAL FAT 11g; SAT FAT 3g; CHOLESTEROL 48mg; SODIUM 1215mg; FIBER 8g

turkey sausage and sauerkraut

assorted mustards

baked beans

applesauce with cinnamon and honey

ginger ale floats

**menu
gameplan**

serves 4

shopping list

Refrigerated prepared sauerkraut

Turkey sausage links, Italian-style

Beer

Apple juice

Caraway seeds

Baked beans

Unsweetened applesauce

Lemon (for juice)

Vanilla ice cream

Ginger ale, preferably Vernor's

from your pantry

Onion

Olive oil

Sugar

Freshly ground black pepper

Assorted mustards

Honey

Ground cinnamon

step 1 make the **turkey sausage and sauerkraut**

step 2 heat the **baked beans**

step 3 prepare the **applesauce with cinnamon and honey**

step 4 make the **ginger ale floats**

step 5 **serve**

luckyforyou Different beers can be used in the sausage recipe for a change in flavor. Try a dark beer for a smokier taste.

"This rendition of sausages and sauerkraut, which is traditionally made with bratwurst, has less fat but is still rich-tasting and very satisfying."

—minutemeals' Chef Hillary

step 1

make the **turkey sausage and sauerkraut**

1 large onion

1 package (16 ounces) refrigerated prepared sauerkraut

1 tablespoon olive oil

12 ounces sweet or hot Italian-style turkey sausage links

1 bottle (12 ounces) beer

1/2 cup apple juice

1/2 teaspoon caraway seeds

1 tablespoon sugar

Freshly ground black pepper to taste

Assorted mustards for serving

1. Thinly slice the onion. Rinse and drain the sauerkraut.

2. In a large saucepan, heat the olive oil over medium heat. Add the turkey sausage, cover, and cook, turning occasionally, for 3 minutes, until browned.

3. Stir in the onion. Cover and cook, stirring once or twice, for 3 minutes. Stir in the sauerkraut, beer, apple juice, caraway seeds, and sugar. Cover and bring to a boil. Reduce the heat to low and partially cover. Simmer for 5 minutes, until the sausage is cooked through and the sauerkraut is steaming. Season with pepper. Keep warm, covered.

step 2

heat the **baked beans**

1 can (16 ounces) baked beans

Put the baked beans in a microwave-safe bowl and microwave on High for 2 minutes, stirring halfway through cooking, until heated through.

step 3

prepare the **applesauce with cinnamon and honey**

1 jar (23 ounces) natural unsweetened applesauce

1 tablespoon honey

1 teaspoon fresh lemon juice

Large pinch of ground cinnamon

Put the applesauce in a medium saucepan and warm over medium heat. Stir in the honey, lemon juice, and cinnamon. Transfer to a serving bowl and keep warm, covered.

step 4

make the **ginger ale floats**

4 scoops vanilla ice cream

2 or 3 bottles chilled ginger ale (preferably Vernor's)

Straws and/or soda spoons for serving

Put a scoop of ice cream into each of 4 tall glasses. Place in the freezer until serving time.

step 5

serve

1. Transfer the sausages and sauerkraut to a platter and serve on dinner plates, with assorted mustards and the baked beans and spiced applesauce as accompaniments.

2. When ready for dessert, pour ginger ale slowly into each of the glasses, covering the ice cream, to the very top. Serve each float with a straw and/or a soda spoon.

Turkey Sausage and Sauerkraut
Single serving is 1/4 of total recipe
CALORIES 198; PROTEIN 13g; CARBS 14g; TOTAL FAT 10g; SAT FAT 2g; CHOLESTEROL 48mg; SODIUM 969mg; FIBER 4g

minute
3 ways

meat menus

meals
to dinner

microwave zucchini boats
with mexican beef stuffing

sunflower tomato salad

cheesecake

serves 4

step	1	make the **microwave zucchini boats with mexican beef stuffing**
step	2	assemble the **sunflower tomato salad**
step	3	**serve**

shopping list

Lean ground beef

Zucchini

Chunky salsa, preferably garlic and cilantro flavored

Frozen or canned corn kernels

Pre-shredded hot pepper Jack cheese

Cherry tomatoes, yellow or red (from the salad bar)

Jarred red and yellow roasted pepper strips

Red wine vinaigrette dressing

Prewashed romaine lettuce

Roasted sunflower seeds

Precut wedges of cheesecake (4)

from your pantry

Chili powder

Ground cumin

Salt and pepper

luckyforyou Traditional stuffed zucchini would take almost an hour to cook. The microwave enables you to serve this dish in record time.

"This stuffing works equally well in bell pepper halves or hollowed-out tomatoes. Or use it to fill soft or hard tacos."

—minutemeals' Chef Paul

step 1

make the **microwave zucchini boats with mexican beef stuffing**

12 ounces lean ground beef

3 or 4 zucchini (about 2 pounds total weight)

1 cup prepared chunky salsa, preferably garlic and cilantro flavored

1 teaspoon chili powder

1 teaspoon ground cumin

1 cup frozen or drained canned corn kernels

1 1/2 cups pre-shredded hot pepper Jack cheese

1. Crumble the beef into a large nonstick skillet and place over medium-high heat. Cook, breaking up the meat and stirring occasionally, for 5 minutes. Drain off the fat, if necessary.

2. Meanwhile, trim the zucchini and halve each lengthwise. Scrape out the seeded centers with a spoon and discard. Place the shells in a large (11 × 7-inch) microwave-safe baking dish and cover with vented plastic wrap. Microwave on High for 8 to 10 minutes, or until almost tender when pierced with a fork.

3. Meanwhile, stir the salsa, chili powder, cumin, and corn into the beef. Cook, stirring often, for 3 minutes. Remove the pan from the heat and stir in half of the cheese. Spoon the beef mixture into the zucchini halves and around them and sprinkle with the remaining cheese. Cover with a sheet of waxed paper and microwave on High for 2 minutes, or until the cheese is melted.

step 2

assemble the **sunflower tomato salad**

3/4 cup small yellow or red cherry tomatoes

1/2 cup jarred red and yellow roasted pepper strips

2 to 3 tablespoons red wine vinaigrette dressing

1 bag (5 ounces) prewashed romaine lettuce

Salt and pepper to taste

3 tablespoons roasted sunflower seeds

1. Rinse the cherry tomatoes and pat dry.

2. Halve the tomatoes and place them in a salad bowl. Add the pepper strips and vinaigrette. Mound the salad greens on top; do not toss until serving time.

step 3

serve

1. Toss the salad, season with salt and pepper, and sprinkle the sunflower seeds over the top. Place the bowl on the table.

2. Serve the stuffed zucchini directly from the baking dish.

3. When ready for dessert, plate the slices of cheesecake and serve.

Microwave Zucchini Boats with Mexican Beef Stuffing
Single serving is 1/4 of total recipe
CALORIES 341; PROTEIN 28g; CARBS 20g; TOTAL FAT 18g; SAT FAT 8g; CHOLESTEROL 75mg; SODIUM 743mg; FIBER 4g

beef, ramen noodle, and vegetable stew

olive pesto spread with crusty whole-grain bread

butter pecan ice cream and pecan shortbread cookies

menu gameplan

shopping list

Lean ground beef

Red onion

Italian green beans, frozen

Diced tomatoes with roasted garlic

Instant ramen noodle soup

White beans, canned

Prepared pesto

Kalamata or brine-cured olives, pitted

Crusty whole-grain bread

Butter pecan ice cream

Pecan shortbread cookies

from your pantry

Worcestershire sauce

Dried Italian herb seasoning

Salt and pepper

serves 4

beforeyoustart

Bring 2 cups water, covered, to a boil for the stew.

step **1** cook the **beef, ramen noodle, and vegetable stew**

step **2** make the **olive pesto spread**

step **3** **serve**

headsup Feel free to substitute ground chicken or pork, bulk break-fast pork sausage, or cut-up leftover meat for the ground beef. Use your favorite frozen vegetables for the beans. Or turn this stew into a hearty soup by making it in a saucepan and adding 2 cans of broth.

"This skillet recipe is a dandy meal in itself, an all-in-one. Make it even simpler and omit the olive spread. Serve butter!"

—minutemeals' Chef Paul

step 1

cook the **beef, ramen noodle, and vegetable stew**

12 ounces lean ground beef

1 medium red onion

1 package (10 ounces) frozen Italian green beans

2 cups boiling water

1 can (15 ounces) diced tomatoes with roasted garlic

2 teaspoons Worcestershire sauce

1 teaspoon dried Italian herb seasoning

2 packages (3 ounces each) instant ramen noodle soup

Salt and pepper to taste

1. Place the ground beef in a large deep nonstick skillet over medium-high heat.

2. Chop the onion and add it to the beef. Cook, breaking up the meat with a spoon and stirring occasionally, for 5 minutes, or until the meat is no longer pink. Drain off any excess fat through a strainer.

3. Meanwhile, microwave the frozen green beans in a microwave-safe bowl on High for 6 minutes, or according to the directions on the package.

4. Stir the boiling water, undrained tomatoes, green beans, Worcestershire sauce, and Italian seasoning into the meat mixture and bring to a simmer. Meanwhile, open the packages of instant soup and discard the seasoning packets.

5. Break up the noodles from both packets into about 6 pieces each, add them to the skillet, and stir to submerge them in the liquid. Cover the skillet and cook, stirring occasionally, for 5 minutes, or until the noodles are tender. Season with salt and pepper.

step 2

make the **olive pesto spread with crusty whole-grain bread**

1 cup canned white beans

2 tablespoons prepared pesto

3 tablespoons pitted kalamata or brine-cured olives

1 small crusty whole-grain bread loaf

1. Rinse the beans and drain well. Drain the pesto of excess oil.

2. Place the beans, pesto, and olives in a mini-processor. Using on/off pulses, process just until the olives are chopped and the beans are puréed. Scrape the spread into a serving bowl.

3. Cut 8 slices of the bread and place in a bread basket.

step 3

serve

1. Stir the stew to combine it. Add additional water, if desired. (The noodles will absorb water as they stand.) Ladle the stew into soup bowls and serve.

2. Serve the olive pesto with the bread.

3. When ready for dessert, scoop the ice cream into 4 dessert bowls, garnish each bowl with 1 or 2 pecan shortbread cookies, and serve.

Beef, Ramen Noodle, and Vegetable Stew
Single serving is $1/4$ of total recipe
CALORIES 323; PROTEIN 20g; CARBS 49g; TOTAL FAT 7g; SAT FAT 2g; CHOLESTEROL 23mg; SODIUM 710mg; FIBER 9g

moroccan beef and squash
with couscous
steamed broccoli with tapenade dressing
orange wedges

menu
gameplan

shopping list

Couscous

Lean ground beef

Zucchini

Yellow squash

Diced tomatoes with roasted garlic

No-salt-added tomato sauce

Broccoli florets
(from the salad bar or produce department)

Kalamata olives, pitted

Red wine vinaigrette dressing

Navel oranges (4)

from your pantry

Sugar

Curry powder

Ground cumin

Ground ginger

Ground cinnamon

Salt and pepper

serves 4

| step | 1 | prepare the **moroccan beef and squash** |

| step | 2 | cook the **steamed broccoli with tapenade dressing** |

| step | 3 | **serve** |

headsup Use 90% lean ground beef here. You won't have to use valuable time to drain it, and you'll save on calories and have less waste, too.

"Use the intriguing combination of Moroccan spices in this pasta dish on vegetables, fish, and poultry, too."

—minutemeals' Chef Paul

step 1

prepare the **moroccan beef and squash with couscous**

1 box (10 ounces) plain couscous, such as Near East brand

12 ounces lean ground beef

1 medium zucchini (about 8 ounces)

1 medium yellow summer squash (about 8 ounces)

1 can (15 ounces) diced tomatoes with roasted garlic

1 can (8 ounces) no-salt-added tomato sauce

1 teaspoon sugar

1 teaspoon curry powder

1/2 teaspoon ground cumin

1/4 teaspoon ground ginger

1/4 teaspoon ground cinnamon

Salt and pepper to taste

1. Prepare the couscous according to the directions on the package. Let stand while making the beef mixture.

2. Cook the Moroccan beef: Crumble the beef into a large nonstick skillet over medium-high heat. Cook, stirring often, for 5 minutes, until the meat is lightly browned. Drain off any fat, if necessary.

3. Meanwhile, trim the zucchini and yellow squash and cut each into 1/2-inch pieces. Add to skillet with the undrained tomatoes, tomato sauce, sugar, curry powder, cumin, ginger, and cinnamon. Bring to a simmer and cook, stirring occasionally, for 5 to 7 minutes, or until the squash is tender and the flavors have blended. (Add a little water or tomato juice if the stew looks very thick.) Season with salt and pepper. Keep warm, covered.

step 2

cook the **steamed broccoli with tapenade dressing**

12 ounces broccoli (1 bag) florets (or mixed broccoli and cauliflower florets)

1/4 cup pitted kalamata olives (about 12)

1/4 cup store-bought red wine vinaigrette dressing

2 tablespoons water

1/4 teaspoon ground cumin

1. Place the broccoli florets in a steamer basket set over boiling water, cover, and steam for 4 to 5 minutes, or until just tender. Place on a serving plate.

2. Meanwhile, combine the olives, vinaigrette, water, and cumin in a mini-processor or blender and process until smooth. Spoon over broccoli. Place the bowl on the table.

step 3

serve

1. Serve the Moroccan beef and couscous directly from the skillet on 4 dinner plates.

2. Serve the broccoli with the couscous combination or on 4 separate plates.

3. When ready for dessert, slice the oranges into wedges and place them on a plate. Serve with 4 dessert plates.

Moroccan Beef and Squash with Couscous
Single serving is 1/4 of total recipe

CALORIES 451; PROTEIN 25g; CARBS 71g; TOTAL FAT 7g; SAT FAT 2g; CHOLESTEROL 23mg; SODIUM 734mg; FIBER 7g

steaks pizzaiola

orzo with olive oil

green beans

kiwi and berry yogurt parfaits

menu
gameplan

shopping list

Green pepper

Boneless New York beef strip steaks

Diced tomatoes

Orzo

Trimmed green beans

Kiwi fruit

Blueberries

Strawberries

Low-fat vanilla yogurt

from your pantry

Onion

Garlic

Salt and pepper

Olive oil

Dried Italian herb seasoning

Crushed red pepper flakes

Grated Parmesan cheese

serves 4

step **1** make the **steaks pizzaiola**

step **2** cook the **orzo with olive oil**

step **3** cook the **green beans**

step **4** prepare the **kiwi and berry yogurt parfaits**

step **5** **serve**

headsup If you ask the butcher to cut the steaks uniformly ¹/₂ to 1 inch thick, you will be much better able to time for doneness.

"Pizzaiola sauce is full of flavor and great with steak, but it works on chicken and fish, too. Make it ahead and freeze it."
—minutemeals' Chef Hillary

step 1

make the **steaks pizzaiola**

1 small onion

1 small green pepper

4 garlic cloves

4 boneless New York beef strip steaks (6 to 8 ounces each)

Salt and pepper to taste

1 tablespoon olive oil

2 cans (14$\frac{1}{2}$ ounces each) drained diced tomatoes

$\frac{1}{2}$ teaspoon crushed Italian herb seasoning

$\frac{1}{4}$ teaspoon crushed red pepper flakes

1. Chop the onion and green pepper. Thinly slice the garlic.

2. Heat a large cast-iron skillet over high heat. Season the steaks with salt and pepper, add them to the pan, and cook for 5 minutes per side for medium-rare, or to desired doneness. Transfer the steaks to a large plate, cover loosely with aluminum foil, and keep warm.

3. In a large nonstick skillet, heat the olive oil over high heat. Add the chopped onion and green pepper and garlic and stir to coat with the oil. Reduce the heat to medium, cover, and cook for 3 to 5 minutes, or until the vegetables are nearly tender.

4. Stir in the drained tomatoes, Italian seasoning, and pepper flakes. Cover and simmer for 5 to 7 minutes, or until sauce has thickened slightly.

step 2

cook the **orzo with olive oil**

2 quarts water

Salt to taste

1 cup orzo

2 tablespoons grated Parmesan cheese

1 tablespoon olive oil

Salt and pepper to taste

Pour the water into a large saucepan, salt lightly, and cover. Bring to a boil over high heat. Add the orzo, stir to separate, and cook according to the directions on the package until tender. Drain well in a colander and transfer to a serving bowl. Stir in the Parmesan, olive oil, and salt and pepper. Keep warm, covered.

step 3

cook the **green beans**

Salt to taste

$\frac{1}{2}$ pound trimmed green beans

Fill a medium saucepan with 1 inch cold water, salt lightly, and add the beans. Cover and bring to a boil over high heat. Cook for 3 to 5 minutes, or until tender. Drain and transfer to a serving bowl. Place the bowl on the table.

step 4

prepare the **kiwi and berry yogurt parfaits**

2 kiwi fruit

1 cup fresh blueberries

1 pint ripe strawberries

1 container (8 ounces) low-fat vanilla yogurt

1. Peel and thinly slice the kiwi fruit. Rinse and pick over the blueberries. Rinse, hull, and slice the strawberries. Combine all the fruit in a bowl.

2. Divide the fruit among 4 dessert bowls.

step 5

serve

1. Place 1 steak on each of 4 dinner plates and top with some of the pizzaiola sauce. Serve the remaining sauce at the table.

2. Spoon a serving of the orzo alongside each steak and serve.

3. When ready for dessert, top the fruit in each bowl with some of the yogurt and serve.

Steak Pizzaiola
Single serving is $\frac{1}{4}$ of total recipe
CALORIES 511; PROTEIN 33g; CARBS 13g; TOTAL FAT 36g; SAT FAT 14g; CHOLESTEROL 101mg; SODIUM 486mg; FIBER 4g

spicy thai beef
on crisp salad
warm flour tortillas
coconut cake with papaya

menu
gameplan

shopping list

Boneless beef top round steak

Cilantro

Limes (for juice)

Chili paste with garlic

Flour tortillas (10-inch diameter)

Prewashed colorful crisp mixed salad greens, such as a Dole® blend

Thai fish sauce or soy sauce

Ripe papaya

Coconut cake

from the salad bar

Cucumber slices

Red onion slices

from your pantry

Nonstick vegetable cooking spray

Garlic

Salt

Sugar

Vegetable oil

serves 4

beforeyoustart
Preheat the broiler.

step	1	cook the **spicy thai beef**
step	2	prepare the **warm flour tortillas**
step	3	assemble the **crisp salad**
step	4	prepare the **coconut cake with papaya**
step	5	**serve**

luckyforyou Because these beef strips are cut so thin, they cook in all of 2 minutes!

"Here's an even quicker way to serve this: Skip the salad and serve the beef strips wrapped in large Boston or iceberg lettuce leaves."

—minutemeals' Chef Hillary

step 1

cook the **spicy thai beef**

Nonstick vegetable cooking spray

1 pound boneless beef top round steak

1/2 cup cilantro sprigs

4 garlic cloves

2 tablespoons fresh lime juice (2 limes)

1 tablespoon water

1 tablespoon chili paste with garlic, or less to taste

1 teaspoon salt

1. Preheat the broiler. Line a broiler pan with aluminum foil. Spray the broiler-pan rack with nonstick cooking spray.

2. Trim any fat from the steak. Cut the steak in half lengthwise, then cut across the grain into 1/8-inch-thick strips.

3. In a food processor, put the cilantro, garlic, lime juice, water, chili paste, and salt. Process to a smooth paste, adding a little more water if necessary. Scrape into a large bowl. Add the steak strips and toss to coat. Marinate for 2 minutes.

4. Arrange the steak strips in a single layer on the prepared pan rack. Broil 4 inches from the heat for 1 minute on each side for medium rare, or to desired doneness. Remove from the broiler and transfer the strips to a bowl.

step 2

prepare the **warm flour tortillas**

4 flour tortillas (10-inch diameter)

Wrap the stack of tortillas loosely in aluminum foil and heat them in a toaster oven at 350°F for 5 to 8 minutes. Transfer to a napkin-lined basket and cover to keep warm. Place the basket on the table.

step 3

assemble the **crisp salad**

1 bag (8 ounces) prewashed colorful crisp mixed salad greens

1 1/2 cups cucumber slices

1/2 cup red onion slices

1/4 cup fresh lime juice (3 or 4 large limes)

1 tablespoon Thai fish sauce or soy sauce

2 teaspoons sugar

1 tablespoon vegetable oil

1. In a large salad bowl, combine the greens, cucumbers, and red onion slices.

2. In a small bowl, stir together the lime juice, fish sauce, sugar, and vegetable oil until the sugar is dissolved. Pour the dressing over the salad and toss.

step 4

prepare the **coconut cake with papaya**

1 ripe papaya

1 store-bought small coconut cake

Peel the papaya with a vegetable peeler, cut it in half, and scoop out the seeds with a small spoon. Cut the papaya into slices and place them in a bowl.

step 5

serve

1. Top the salad with the beef strips, adding any juice that has accumulated in the bowl. Toss well and divide the beef and salad evenly among 4 dinner plates. Serve with the warm tortillas.

2. When ready for dessert, cut the coconut cake into 4 slices, place each on a dessert plate, and garnish with papaya slices. Serve.

Spicy Thai Beef on Crisp Salad
Single serving is 1/4 of total recipe
CALORIES 173; PROTEIN 26g; CARBS 2g;
TOTAL FAT 6g; SAT FAT 2g; CHOLESTEROL 75mg;
SODIUM 640mg; FIBER 0g

steaks
with shallot and herb butter

new potatoes with dill and sour cream

steak house salads

brownies à la mode

menu gameplan

serves 4

step	1	cook the **new potatoes**
step	2	cook the **steaks**
step	3	assemble the **steak house salads**
step	4	prepare the **brownies à la mode**
step	5	**serve**

shopping list

Small thin-skinned potatoes

Reduced-fat sour cream

Fresh dill

Shallots

Fresh parsley

Chives

Minute steaks

Beefsteak tomatoes

Sweet onion, such as Vidalia

Sweet-and-sour or Roquefort salad dressing

Vanilla fudge ice cream

Brownies

from your pantry

Dried dill seed (optional)

Salt

Freshly ground black pepper

Butter

Beef broth

Red wine vinegar, red wine, or brandy

headsup Minute steaks will be most tender if cooked medium-rare. Scoring little slits into the edge of the steaks with the tip of a sharp paring knife will help to tenderize the meat.

"To me, this is the perfect celebration dinner. It's sophisticated without being fussy. Order up a birthday cake and you're in business!"

—minutemeals' Chef Hillary

step 1

cook the **new potatoes**

1¼ pounds small thin-skinned potatoes

¼ teaspoon dried dill seed (optional)

Salt to taste

3 tablespoons reduced-fat sour cream

2 teaspoons snipped fresh dill

Freshly ground black pepper to taste

1. Cut the potatoes into quarters.

2. Put the potatoes and dill seed, if using, in a medium saucepan. Add ½ inch cold water and salt to taste. Cover and bring to a boil over high heat. Reduce the heat to medium and cook, partially covered, 5 to 6 minutes, or until tender. Drain the potatoes and transfer to a serving dish.

3. Add the sour cream, fresh dill, and salt and pepper and toss gently. Put the bowl on the table.

step 2

cook the **steaks**

2 large shallots

2 tablespoons chopped fresh parsley

2 teaspoons snipped chives or thinly sliced green part of scallion

4 minute steaks (6 ounces each)

Salt and pepper to taste

2 tablespoons butter

½ cup beef broth

2 tablespoons red wine vinegar, red wine, or brandy

1. Chop the shallots. Chop enough parsley to measure 2 tablespoons. Snip enough chives or slice enough green part of scallion to measure 2 teaspoons.

2. Heat a large cast-iron skillet or other heavy skillet over high heat until it feels warm when you hold your hand above it. Season the steaks with salt and pepper. Add the steaks to the hot skillet and cook for 1 minute per side for rare, or to desired doneness. Transfer the steaks to a serving platter and cover loosely to keep warm.

3. Reduce the heat to medium. Add the butter to the skillet and when it melts stir in the shallots. Cook, stirring, for 2 minutes, or until just golden. Add the broth and vinegar or wine, cover and bring to a boil. Reduce the heat and simmer for 2 minutes, until slightly reduced. Remove the pan from the heat. Pour in any steak juices that have accumulated on the plate and stir in the chives and parsley. Spoon over the steaks and cover to keep warm.

step 3

assemble the **steak house salads**

4 medium beefsteak tomatoes

1 large sweet onion, such as Vidalia

Sweet-and-sour or store-bought Roquefort salad dressing

Salt and pepper to taste

1. Rinse the tomatoes, pat dry, and slice. Thickly slice the onion.

2. Place 1 sliced tomato on each of 4 salad plates and insert 1 or 2 slices of onion among the tomato slices. Drizzle each salad with dressing and season with salt and pepper. Place the salads on the table.

step 4

prepare the **brownies à la mode**

1 pint vanilla fudge ice cream

4 store-bought brownies

1. Remove the ice cream from the freezer to soften slightly.

2. Place a brownie on each of 4 dessert plates.

step 5

serve

1. Serve the steaks with the shallot and herb butter from the platter with the potatoes and salads as accompaniments.

2. When ready for dessert, place a scoop of ice cream on each brownie and serve.

Steaks with Shallot and Herb Butter
Single serving is ¼ of total recipe
CALORIES 489; PROTEIN 21g; CARBS 2g; TOTAL FAT 44g; SAT FAT 19g; CHOLESTEROL 112mg; SODIUM 345mg; FIBER 0g

sesame garlic beef stir-fry
scallion noodles
ambrosial pineapple

menu gameplan

shopping list

Shredded sweetened coconut

Vermicelli or angel hair pasta

Scallions

Gingerroot

Beef for stir-fry

Stringed snow peas

Prepared garlic-ginger stir-fry sauce

from the salad bar

Cubed pineapple or juice-packed canned pineapple

Broccoli florets
(or from the produce department)

Pre-shredded carrots
(or from the produce department)

from your pantry

Orange juice

Salt

Toasted sesame oil

Garlic

Sesame seeds

Vegetable oil

serves 4

beforeyoustart
Bring water in a large pot, covered, to a boil over high heat to cook the pasta.

step **1** assemble the **ambrosial pineapple**

step **2** cook the **scallion noodles**

step **3** cook the **sesame garlic beef stir-fry**

step **4** **serve**

headsup Since beef stir-fry is cut from the round, which is very lean, be sure not to overcook it or it will be tough. If the strips are longer than 3 inches, cut them in half.

"In addition to being a quick way to cook, a homemade stir-fry also allows the chef to keep the oil used to a minimum."
—minutemeals' Chef Sarah

step 1

assemble the **ambrosial pineapple**

3 cups cubed fresh pineapple or juice-packed canned chunks

2 tablespoons orange juice

2 tablespoons shredded sweetened coconut

In a medium bowl, combine the pineapple and orange juice. Divide among 4 dessert dishes. Sprinkle with coconut. Let stand until serving time.

step 2

cook the **scallion noodles**

4 quarts water

1 teaspoon salt

1/2 pound vermicelli or angel hair pasta

2 scallions

1/2-inch piece gingerroot

2 teaspoons toasted sesame oil

1. Pour the water into a large pot, add the salt, and cover. Bring to a boil over high heat. Add the pasta, stir to separate the strands, and cook according to the directions on the package just until *al dente*. Drain well in a colander. Return the pasta to the pot.

2. While the pasta cooks, finely chop the scallions. Finely grate the ginger.

3. Add the scallions, ginger, and sesame oil to the cooked pasta and toss until evenly coated. Cover to keep warm.

step 3

cook the **sesame garlic beef stir-fry**

2 teaspoons minced garlic (2 garlic cloves)

3/4 pound beef for stir-fry

2 tablespoons sesame seeds

1 tablespoon plus 1 teaspoon vegetable oil

3 cups small broccoli florets

1 cup pre-shredded carrots

1 cup packed stringed snow peas

2 tablespoons water

1/4 cup prepared garlic-ginger stir-fry sauce

1. Mince enough garlic to measure 2 teaspoons.

2. In a medium bowl, toss the beef with the sesame seeds until coated.

3. In a large nonstick skillet, heat 1 tablespoon vegetable oil over high heat. Add the beef and cook, stirring constantly, until browned but still pink inside, about 1 minute. Remove the beef to a plate.

4. Heat the remaining 1 teaspoon vegetable oil in the skillet over medium-high heat. Add the broccoli, carrots, snow peas, and garlic and cook, stirring constantly, until the vegetables are tender-crisp, about 2 minutes. Add the water, cover, and cook for 1 to 2 minutes, until the broccoli is tender and bright-colored. Add the stir-fry sauce and beef with any juices that have collected on the plate. Cook, stirring constantly, for 1 minute, or until beef is hot.

step 4

serve

1. Divide the scallion noodles among 4 dinner plates, top with beef stir-fry, and serve.

2. When ready for dessert, serve the ambrosial pineapple.

Sesame Garlic Beef Stir-Fry
Single serving is 1/4 of total recipe
CALORIES 257; PROTEIN 23g; CARBS 13g; TOTAL FAT 13g; SAT FAT 2g; CHOLESTEROL 56mg; SODIUM 206mg; FIBER 4g

☆ beef fajitas
warm corn salad
caramel "flans"

menu
gameplan

shopping list

Vanilla custard-style yogurt

Caramel or butterscotch
ice cream topping

Tomato

Scallion

Frozen or canned corn
kernels

Flour tortillas (7-inch diameter)

Green pepper slices
(from the salad bar)

Beef for stir-fry

Limes (for juice)

Ripe avocados

Salsa

Sour cream (optional)

from your pantry

Brewed coffee

Vinaigrette dressing,
store-bought or homemade

Salt and pepper

Vegetable oil

Mexican or Southwest
seasoning

Prepared hot sauce (optional)

serves 4

beforeyoustart

Preheat the oven to 350°F to heat
the tortillas.

step **1** assemble the **caramel "flans"**

step **2** make the **warm corn salad**

step **3** cook the **beef fajitas**

step **4** **serve**

headsup
Make sure the skillet is hot,
so the beef sears rather than
steams. If the beef stir-fry strips are longer than 3 inches,
cut them in half.

"Beef fajitas are very popular on restaurant menus and can be prepared quickly at home if you use already sliced meat."

—minutemeals' Chef Sarah

step 1

assemble the **caramel "flans"**

4 containers (6 ounces each) vanilla custard-style yogurt

1/3 cup caramel or butterscotch ice cream topping

1 tablespoon brewed coffee

1. Spoon the yogurt into 4 dessert dishes.

2. In a small bowl, combine the caramel sauce and coffee. Drizzle the sauce over the yogurts. Refrigerate.

step 2

make the **warm corn salad**

1 medium tomato

1 scallion

2 tablespoons vinaigrette dressing

2 cups frozen or drained canned corn kernels

Salt and pepper to taste

1. Dice the tomato and slice the scallion.

2. In a large nonstick skillet, combine the vinaigrette and corn and cook over medium heat, stirring frequently, until the corn is hot, about 3 minutes. Remove the pan from the heat. Stir in the tomato and scallion and season with salt and pepper. Spoon into a serving bowl. Cover to keep warm.

step 3

cook the **beef fajitas**

8 (7-inch diameter) flour tortillas

1 1/2 cups green pepper slices

1 tablespoon vegetable oil

1 pound beef for stir-fry

2 teaspoons Mexican or Southwest seasoning

2 tablespoons fresh lime juice (2 limes)

Salt and pepper to taste

2 ripe avocados

1 jar (12 ounces) prepared salsa

Sour cream for serving (optional)

Prepared hot sauce (optional)

1. Preheat the oven to 350°F.

2. Wrap the tortillas in aluminum foil and heat in the oven while you make the filling mixture.

3. Cut the pepper slices in half.

4. Heat the vegetable oil in a large nonstick skillet over high heat. Add the beef, peppers, and Mexican seasoning. Stir-fry until the beef is browned, but still pink inside, about 2 minutes. Stir in the lime juice. Remove the skillet from the heat and season with salt and pepper.

5. Peel and pit the avocados and cut into chunks. Place in a bowl.

6. Spoon the salsa and sour cream, if using, into bowls and put both on the table with the avocado.

step 4

serve

1. Transfer the heated tortillas to a napkin-lined basket, cover, and place on the table.

2. Transfer the beef to a serving bowl and serve at once with the accompaniments, letting diners assemble their own fajitas. Serve with hot sauce at the table, if desired.

3. Serve the corn salad separately or along with the beef in the fajitas.

4. When ready for dessert, serve the flans.

Beef Fajitas
Single serving is 1/4 of total recipe
CALORIES 692; PROTEIN 36g; CARBS 73g; TOTAL FAT 30g; SAT FAT 6g; CHOLESTEROL 63mg; SODIUM 1178mg; FIBER 10g

sloppy joes

deli potato salad
sliced tomatoes and cucumbers
chocolate ice cream pies

menugameplan

shopping list

Chocolate or rocky road ice cream

Individual graham cracker pie shells

Hot fudge sauce

Ripe tomatoes

Prepared potato salad (from the deli counter)

Beef for stir-fry

Tomato chili sauce

Hard or kaiser rolls

from the salad bar

Cucumber slices

Green pepper slices

Red onion slices

from your pantry

Salt and fresh pepper

Rice vinegar

Vegetable or olive oil

Brown sugar

Cider vinegar

serves 4

beforeyoustart

Let the ice cream stand at room temperature until soft enough to scoop.

step	1	assemble the **chocolate ice cream pies**
step	2	plate the **sliced tomatoes, cucumbers** and **deli potato salad**
step	3	make the **sloppy joes**
step	4	**serve**

luckyforyou These sloppy joes can also be made with chicken or pork cut for stir-fry.

"For a change from ground beef, these 'sj's' are made with beef strips, with peppers and onions added for crunch. The sauce couldn't be easier."

—minutemeals' Chef Sarah

step 1

assemble the **chocolate ice cream pies**

1 pint chocolate or rocky road ice cream

4 individual graham cracker pie shells

1/2 cup jarred hot fudge sauce

1. Scoop softened ice cream into each of the pie shells. Place in the freezer until serving time.

2. In a microwave-safe bowl, microwave the hot fudge sauce on High until warm. Keep warm.

step 2

plate the **sliced tomatoes and cucumbers** and **deli potato salad**

4 ripe tomatoes

1 cup cucumber slices

Salt and fresh pepper to taste

Rice vinegar to taste

Prepared potato salad for 4

1. Rinse the tomatoes and pat dry. Cut into thin slices. Arrange the tomatoes around the edge of a round serving platter.

2. Spoon the cucumber slices into the middle of the platter. Season with salt and pepper and drizzle with rice vinegar. Place the platter on the table.

3. Spoon the potato salad into a serving bowl and place on the table.

step 3

make the **sloppy joes**

1 cup green pepper slices

1/2 cup red onion slices

3 teaspoons vegetable or olive oil

1 pound beef for stir-fry

3/4 cup tomato chili sauce

1 tablespoon brown sugar

1 tablespoon cider vinegar

Pepper to taste

4 hard or kaiser rolls

1. Cut the pepper and onion slices in half.

2. In a large deep nonstick skillet, heat 2 teaspoons of the vegetable oil over high heat. Add the beef and stir-fry until no longer pink, about 1 minute. Transfer to a plate.

3. Add the remaining 1 teaspoon oil, peppers and red onions to the skillet. Cook over medium heat, stirring frequently, until tender, about 4 minutes. Stir in any juices that have accumulated from the beef, the chili sauce, brown sugar, vinegar, and pepper. Bring to a boil. Reduce the heat to medium-low and simmer uncovered, stirring occasionally, for 5 minutes.

4. Stir in the beef and simmer, for 1 minute to heat through.

step 4

serve

1. Split the rolls and place a roll on each of 4 dinner plates. Spoon the sloppy joe mixture over them, dividing it equally. Serve at once, with the salads as accompaniments.

2. When ready to serve dessert, drizzle the hot fudge sauce over the ice cream pies and serve on 4 dessert plates, with additional fudge sauce, if desired.

Sloppy Joes
Single serving is 1/4 of total recipe
CALORIES 449; PROTEIN 32g; CARBS 52g; TOTAL FAT 12g; SAT FAT 3g; CHOLESTEROL 75mg; SODIUM 1,800mg; FIBER 2g

ham in cheddar sauce
on english muffins

sliced tomatoes with fresh basil

crisp apples and ripe pears

menu gameplan

shopping list

Supersize English muffins

Fully cooked boneless lower sodium ham steak

Fresh chives or parsley

Pre-shredded Cheddar cheese

Beefsteak tomatoes

Fresh basil

Crisp apples

Ripe pears

from your pantry

Butter

All-purpose flour

Milk

Dry sherry

Salt and pepper

Extra virgin olive oil

Balsamic vinegar

serves 4

step **1** make the **ham in cheddar sauce**

step **2** assemble the **sliced tomatoes with fresh basil**

step **3** **serve**

luckyforyou Clean-up is a breeze: Both the Cheddar sauce and ham cook in the same skillet.

"This makes a heavenly brunch or supper dish. To lower the sodium per serving, use whole-wheat toast points instead of the English muffins."

—minutemeals' Chef Hillary

step 1

make the **ham in cheddar sauce**

4 Supersize English muffins

1 fully cooked boneless ham steak (8 to 10 ounces)

2 tablespoons snipped fresh chives or chopped fresh parsley

2 tablespoons butter

2 tablespoons all-purpose flour

1½ cups milk

1½ cups pre-shredded Cheddar cheese

2 tablespoons dry sherry

1. Preheat the broiler. Meanwhile, split the English muffins. Place the halves on the rack of the broiler pan and broil them about 4 inches from the heat until lightly toasted. Remove and place 1 whole muffin on each of 4 dinner plates.

2. Trim the ham steak and cut it into ½-inch pieces. Snip enough chives or chop enough parsley to measure 2 tablespoons.

3. In a medium nonstick skillet, melt the butter over high heat. When it starts to brown slightly, add the ham and cook, stirring occasionally, about 5 minutes, or until it starts to brown. With a slotted spoon, transfer the ham to a plate, leaving the juices in the pan.

4. Return the skillet to the heat and add the flour to the pan juices. Cook, stirring, for 1 minute. With a wire whisk, slowly whisk in the milk. Bring to a boil, whisking constantly. Reduce the heat to low and simmer the sauce, stirring often, for 3 minutes, or until it thickens slightly. Remove the pan from the heat and whisk in the Cheddar, sherry, and chives, stirring until the cheese is melted. Stir in the ham with any juices that have collected on the plate and stir over low heat until the ham is reheated.

step 2

assemble the **sliced tomatoes with fresh basil**

2 large beefsteak tomatoes

⅓ cup chopped fresh basil

Salt and pepper to taste

1 tablespoon extra virgin olive oil

2 teaspoons balsamic vinegar

1. Rinse the tomatoes and pat dry with paper towels. Rinse the basil leaves, pat dry, and sliver or shred enough to measure ⅓ cup.

2. With a sharp knife, thinly slice the tomatoes and place the slices on a serving platter. Season with salt and pepper. Drizzle with the olive oil and vinegar. Scatter the basil over all. Place the platter on the table.

step 3

serve

1. Spoon a quarter of the ham in cheddar sauce over each toasted muffin and serve with the salad alongside or on separate plates.

2. When ready for dessert, serve the apples and pears in a fruit bowl, with 4 dessert plates and knives, if desired.

Ham in Cheddar Sauce on English Muffins
Single serving is ¼ of total recipe
CALORIES 574; PROTEIN 33g; CARBS 48g;
TOTAL FAT 28g; SAT FAT 16g; CHOLESTEROL 103mg;
SODIUM 1251mg; FIBER 2g

☆ ham steak
with spicy mustard sauce
puréed squash
broccoli florets
caribbean pineapple

menu gameplan

shopping list

Fully cooked reduced-sodium ham steak

Peach or apricot preserves

Juice-packed pineapple rings

Frozen cooked squash

Broccoli florets
(from the salad bar or produce department)

from your pantry

Dijon mustard

White wine vinegar

Cayenne pepper or hot pepper sauce

Dark rum

Dark brown sugar

Butter

Ground cinnamon

Ground nutmeg

Salt and pepper

serves 4

beforeyoustart
Preheat the broiler.

step 1 — cook the **ham steak with spicy mustard sauce**

step 2 — prepare the **caribbean pineapple**

step 3 — cook the **puréed squash**

step 4 — steam the **broccoli florets**

step 5 — **serve**

luckyforyou
The spicy mustard sauce here can be made in advance and works well with grilled chicken and broiled or grilled pork, too.

"What you expect to have with ham—pineapple and mustard—is here, just creatively rearranged, which makes the menu interesting and fun."

—minutemeals' Chef Hillary

step 1

cook the **ham steak with spicy mustard sauce**

1 fully cooked reduced-sodium ham steak (16 ounces)

1/2 cup peach or apricot preserves

1/2 cup Dijon mustard

2 tablespoons white wine vinegar

1/8 to 1/4 teaspoon cayenne pepper or hot pepper sauce

1. Preheat the broiler. Line a broiler pan with aluminum foil.

2. Trim the ham steak, cut it into 4 pieces, and pat them dry with paper towels. Place the pieces on the broiler-pan rack.

3. In a small bowl, stir together the apricot preserves, mustard, vinegar, and cayenne. Brush one-quarter of the sauce over the ham pieces. Broil 4 inches from the heat for 4 minutes. Turn the pieces and brush with some of the sauce. Broil for 4 minutes, until the ham is heated, browned, and glazed. Reserve the remaining mustard sauce.

step 2

prepare the **caribbean pineapple**

1 can (20 ounces) juice-packed pineapple rings

2 tablespoons dark rum or pineapple juice from the can

2 tablespoons dark brown sugar

1. Drain the pineapple, reserving a little of the juice, if desired. Place the pineapple in a serving bowl.

2. In a cup, stir together the rum or pineapple juice and brown sugar until the sugar has dissolved. Pour the mixture over the pineapple, toss gently, and let stand at room temperature until serving time.

step 3

cook the **puréed squash**

2 packages (10 ounces each) frozen cooked squash

1 tablespoon butter

Generous 1/8 teaspoon ground cinnamon

Pinch of ground nutmeg

Heat the squash in the microwave oven according to the directions on the package. When hot, stir in the butter, cinnamon, and nutmeg. Keep warm until serving time.

step 4

steam the **broccoli florets**

4 cups broccoli florets

1 tablespoon butter

Salt and pepper to taste

Pour 1/2 cup water into a medium saucepan. Place the broccoli florets in a vegetable steamer basket and set the basket in the pan. Cover and bring to a boil over high heat. Steam until the florets are crisp-tender, about 5 to 7 minutes. Remove the basket, turn the florets into a serving bowl, and add the butter. Toss gently until melted. Season with salt and pepper. Place the bowl on the table.

step 5

serve

1. Place a piece of ham on each of 4 dinner plates. Transfer the remaining mustard sauce to a serving bowl to pass at the table.

2. Spoon some of the squash alongside the ham on each plate and serve with the broccoli florets as an accompaniment.

3. When ready for dessert, serve the pineapple with plenty of the juice in 4 dessert bowls.

Ham Steak with Spicy Mustard Sauce
Single serving is 1/4 of total recipe

CALORIES 301; PROTEIN 26g; CARBS 32g; TOTAL FAT 9g; SAT FAT 2g; CHOLESTEROL 60mg; SODIUM 1872mg; FIBER 1g

corn and ham chowder

pumpernickel bread, cheddar cheese, and pickles

warm spiced apple cider

oatmeal cookies, cinnamon-sugar donuts or rugalach

shopping list

Lemon

Orange

Unsweetened apple cider

Cinnamon sticks

Celery

Creamed corn

Fully cooked ham steak

Red pepper (optional)

Frozen corn

Pumpernickel bread, sliced

Extra-sharp Cheddar cheese

Bread and butter pickles

Oatmeal cookies, cinnamon-sugar old-fashioned donuts or rugalach

from your pantry

Brown sugar

Ground cinnamon

Onion

Butter

Milk

Fat-free reduced-sodium chicken broth

Bay leaf

Salt and pepper

Ground nutmeg

Cayenne pepper

serves 4

step **1** prepare the **warmed spiced apple cider**

step **2** make the **corn and ham chowder**

step **3** plate the **pumpernickel bread, cheddar cheese, and pickles**

step **4** **serve**

luckyforyou Most canned creamed corn contains no preservatives or additives, making it one of the more appealing convenience items on the supermarket shelf.

"This is a nice meal for a cold weeknight supper. To fill out the menu, serve a selection of cheeses and/or a platter of fruit."

—minutemeals' Chef Miriam

step 1

prepare the **warm spiced apple cider**

1 lemon

1 orange

4 cups unsweetened apple cider

1 tablespoon brown sugar

$^1/_8$ teaspoon ground cinnamon

4 cinnamon sticks or
4 sour apple candy sticks

1. Cut 2 thin slices from the lemon and the orange and place them in a medium saucepan. Add the cider, brown sugar, and cinnamon. Warm over low heat until hot. Cover to keep warm.

2. Place 1 cinnamon stick or sour apple candy sticks in each of 4 mugs.

step 2

make the **corn and ham chowder**

1 small onion

2 stalks celery plus $^1/_4$ cup celery leaves

2 tablespoons butter

2 cups milk

1 can (14$^3/_4$ ounces) creamed corn

1 cup fat-free reduced-sodium chicken broth

1 bay leaf

1 fully cooked ham steak (8 ounces)

2 tablespoons diced red pepper for garnish (optional)

1 package (10 ounces) frozen corn

Salt and black pepper to taste

Pinch ground nutmeg

Cayenne pepper to taste

1. Coarsely chop the onion and celery stalks.

2. In a large heavy saucepan or Dutch oven, melt the butter over medium-high heat. Stir in the chopped onion and celery and cook, stirring occasionally, for 4 minutes.

3. Stir in the milk, creamed corn, chicken broth, and bay leaf. Cover and bring to a boil. Reduce the heat to medium, and simmer, uncovered, for 10 minutes.

4. Meanwhile, trim and dice the ham into $^1/_2$-inch chunks. Barely chop the celery leaves. Dice the red pepper, if using.

5. Add the ham, celery leaves, and frozen corn to the soup and simmer for 5 minutes, until heated through. Season with salt, black pepper, nutmeg, and cayenne.

step 3

plate the **pumpernickel bread, cheddar cheese, and pickles**

1 loaf sliced pumpernickel bread

1 wedge (6 to 8 ounces) extra-sharp Cheddar cheese

Bread and butter pickles

Arrange the bread and cheese on a cutting board. Place the pickles in a bowl and set the board and bowl on the table.

step 4

serve

1. Ladle the chowder into 4 large bowls and garnish with diced red pepper, if desired.

2. Serve the bread, Cheddar, and pickles with the chowder.

3. Serve the warm cider in the prepared mugs. Plate the cookies with the donuts or rugalach, or cookies (or all 3) and serve with the cider.

Corn and Ham Chowder
Single serving is $^1/_4$ of total recipe
CALORIES 350; PROTEIN 20g; CARBS 42g; TOTAL FAT 14g; SAT FAT 7g; CHOLESTEROL 59mg; SODIUM 1278mg; FIBER 4g

☆ cheese-stuffed pork chops

honey-glazed baby carrots

tossed greens vinaigrette

ripe pears with caramel sauce

menu gameplan

shopping list

Oil-cured sun-dried tomatoes

Scallion

Boneless loin pork chops

Swiss or fontina cheese

Baby carrots

Lemon (for juice)

Prewashed spring or baby greens

Pecans

Ripe pears

Caramel sauce

from your pantry

Bread crumbs

Grainy mustard

Olive oil

Honey

Butter

Ground cinnamon

Ground allspice (optional)

Vinaigrette dressing, store-bought or homemade

serves 4

step **1** cook the **cheese-stuffed pork chops**

step **2** cook the **honey-glazed baby carrots**

step **3** assemble the **tossed greens vinaigrette**

step **4** prepare the **ripe pears with caramel sauce**

step **5** **serve**

luckyforyou This stuffing works well in large skinless boneless chicken breasts, too.

"These chops are a great do-ahead entree. Just cut the pockets and make the stuffing up to 1 day in advance, then refrigerate both separately."

—minutemeals' Chef Paul

step 1

cook the **cheese-stuffed pork chops**

1 tablespoon chopped oil-cured sun-dried tomatoes

1 scallion

4 boneless loin pork chops, each about 1/2 inch thick (about 1 1/2 pounds total weight)

3/4 cup shredded Swiss or fontina cheese

2 tablespoons dried bread crumbs

1 tablespoon grainy mustard

1 tablespoon olive oil

1. Drain the sun-dried tomatoes and chop enough to measure 1 tablespoon. Chop the scallion. With the blade of a sharp knife, cut a pocket horizontally in each of the pork chops, cutting from the bone side to the fat side. Do not cut all the way through. Shred enough cheese to measure 3/4 cup.

2. In a small bowl, stir together the cheese, tomatoes, bread crumbs, mustard, and scallion. Spoon some of the stuffing into the pocket in each chop and secure the opening with a wooden toothpick. Press down on the chop to even the filling.

3. In a large nonstick skillet, heat the olive oil over medium-low heat until hot. Add the chops without crowding, cover, and cook for 5 minutes. Turn the chops, cover, and cook for 5 minutes more. Turn again and cook, uncovered, for 2 minutes, or until cooked through

and the juices run clear when pricked with a fork. Remove the skillet from the heat.

step 2

cook the **honey-glazed baby carrots**

1 bag (16 ounces) baby carrots

2 tablespoons honey

1 tablespoon butter

1/4 teaspoon ground cinnamon, or to taste

1/8 teaspoon ground allspice (optional)

1 teaspoon lemon juice

1. Place the carrots in a medium saucepan. Add water to cover, cover the pan, and bring to a boil over high heat. Boil for 8 minutes, or just until the carrots are tender. Drain well.

2. Return the carrots to the pan and add the honey, butter, cinnamon, and allspice, if using. Cook, tossing gently, for 2 minutes, or until glazed. Keep warm, covered.

step 3

assemble the **tossed greens vinaigrette**

1 bag (5 ounces) prewashed spring or baby greens

1/4 cup vinaigrette dressing

Place the greens in a salad bowl, add the vinaigrette, and toss gently. Place the bowl on the table.

step 4

prepare the **ripe pears with caramel sauce**

3 tablespoons pecans

2 ripe pears, such as Bartlett or Bosc

1/4 cup jarred caramel sauce, at room temperature

1. In a toaster oven, toast the pecans at 350°F for 5 minutes, stirring once, until fragrant. Remove, cool, and chop.

2. Core each pear and slice. Divide the slices among 4 dessert plates and drizzle with the caramel sauce. Set aside until serving time.

step 5

serve

1. Add the lemon juice to the carrots and toss.

2. Place a pork chop on each of 4 dinner plates and add a serving of carrots alongside. Serve, with the tossed greens as an accompaniment.

3. When ready for dessert, sprinkle each serving of pears with chopped pecans. Serve, with additional caramel sauce, if desired.

Cheese-Stuffed Pork Chops
Single serving is 1/4 of total recipe
CALORIES 401; PROTEIN 37g; CARBS 3g; TOTAL FAT 26g; SAT FAT 11g; CHOLESTEROL 112mg; SODIUM 818mg; FIBER 0g

pork chops
with savory sour cream sauce

buttered egg noodles with poppy seeds
steamed baby carrots
cantaloupe with cookies

shopping list

Egg noodles

Fresh parsley

Boneless pork loin chops

Regular or reduced-fat
sour cream (do not use fat-free)

Baby carrots

Cut-up cantaloupe
(from the salad bar or produce
department)

Crisp chocolate cookies

from your pantry

Salt and pepper

Butter

Poppy seeds

Cornstarch

Dry white wine

Fat-free reduced-sodium
chicken broth

Dijon mustard

serves 4

beforeyoustart

Bring a large pot of water, covered, to a boil over high heat to cook the noodles.

| step | 1 | cook the **buttered egg noodles with poppy seeds** |

| step | 2 | cook the **pork chops with savory sour cream sauce** |

| step | 3 | cook the **steamed baby carrots** |

| step | 4 | **serve** |

heads up

Remember to remove the pan from the heat before adding the sour cream to the sauce base. Otherwise you run the risk of the sour cream curdling. The options are full-fat sour cream or reduced-fat. Fat-free won't do.

"This chop recipe is a good example of how best to cook today's leaner pork—carefully but quickly. The sauce is pure comfort."

—minutemeals' Chef Ruth

step 1

cook the **buttered egg noodles with poppy seeds**

3 quarts water

Salt to taste

8 ounces egg noodles

1 tablespoon butter

1 tablespoon poppy seeds

Pour the water into a large pan, salt lightly, and cover. Bring to a boil over high heat. Add the noodles, stir to separate, and cook according to the directions on the package until *al dente*. Drain in a colander, return to the pan, and add the butter and poppy seeds. Stir until the butter is melted. Keep warm, covered.

step 2

cook the **pork chops with savory sour cream sauce**

2 teaspoons cornstarch

1/3 cup dry white wine (or omit wine and use 2/3 cup chicken broth)

1/3 cup fat-free reduced-sodium chicken broth

2 tablespoons Dijon mustard

2 tablespoons chopped fresh parsley

4 boneless pork loin chops (about 1 1/4 pounds total weight)

Salt and pepper to taste

2/3 cup regular or reduced-fat sour cream

1. In a small saucepan, whisk the cornstarch together with the wine and broth (or only broth). Add the mustard, and whisk until smooth. Chop enough parsley to measure 2 tablespoons.

2. Place the pork chops in a large nonstick skillet over medium-high heat. Season with salt and pepper. Cook until the chops are well browned on the first side, about 5 minutes. Turn and brown the second side, about 3 to 4 minutes. Remove the pan from the heat.

3. While the chops are cooking, place the saucepan with the broth mixture over medium heat. Bring to a boil, stirring constantly, and simmer until slightly thickened, about 3 minutes. Season with salt and pepper. Remove from the heat and stir in the sour cream and parsley until blended. Cover to keep warm.

step 3

cook the **steamed baby carrots**

1/2 cup water

1 bag (16 ounces) baby carrots

1 tablespoon butter (optional)

Salt and pepper to taste

Pour the water into a saucepan with a tight-fitting lid. Place the carrots in a steamer basket and place the basket in the saucepan. Cover, bring to a boil over medium heat, reduce the heat to low, and

steam until the carrots are tender, about 10 minutes. Turn the carrots into a serving bowl, add the butter, if desired, and season with salt and pepper. Place the bowl on the table.

step 4

serve

1. Place 1 pork chop on each of 4 dinner plates. Add a serving of noodles next to the chops. Spoon some of the sour cream sauce over the chops and noodles and serve at once with the carrots as an accompaniment.

2. When ready for dessert, divide the cantaloupe among 4 dessert plates and garnish each serving with a chocolate cookie or two. Serve, with the remaining cookies, if desired.

Pork Chops with Savory Sour Cream Sauce
Single serving is 1/4 of total recipe

CALORIES 317; PROTEIN 34g; CARBS 4g; TOTAL FAT 18g; SAT FAT 8g; CHOLESTEROL 109mg; SODIUM 505mg; FIBER 0g

broiled pork chops
with curried chutney sauce

basmati rice with cashews
tomato and cucumber salad
icy watermelon and meringue cookies

menu
gameplan

serves 4

shopping list

Basmati rice

Cashews or peanuts

Boneless pork chops

Mango or peach chutney

Mild curry paste concentrate for sauces

Red globe tomatoes or cherry tomatoes

Baby spinach leaves

Cucumber salad (from the salad bar)

Ranch salad dressing

Watermelon cubes for 4 (from the produce department)

Meringue cookies

from your pantry

Salt and pepper

Nonstick cooking spray

beforeyoustart

Preheat the broiler. Place the watermelon cubes in the freezer until serving time.

step 1 cook the **basmati rice with cashews**

step 2 cook the **pork chops with curried chutney sauce**

step 3 assemble the **tomato and cucumber salad**

step 4 serve

 **heads**up Concentrated curry sauce pastes vary greatly in intensity of flavor. This recipe calls for mild curry paste, but if you have a spicier "vindaloo" style of curry paste on hand from an Indian market, start with a smaller amount and add it judiciously to taste. Curry paste has an intensity of color as well as flavor, so hasten to clean up spills immediately lest they stain countertops, cutting boards, and aprons.

"The combination of the curry-flavored chops and cool cucumber salad is a winner. The menu seems far more involved than it actually is."

—minutemeals' Chef Ruth

step 1

cook the **basmati rice with cashews**

1 cup basmati rice

Water

Salt to taste (optional)

1/2 cup salted cashews or peanuts

1. Cook the basmati rice in a medium saucepan according to the directions and for the time directed on the package. Keep warm.

2. While the rice cooks, coarsely chop the nuts.

step 2

cook the **pork chops with curried chutney sauce**

Nonstick cooking spray

8 thin boneless pork chops, each about 1/2 inch thick (about 1 1/4 pounds total weight), or 4 1-inch-thick chops

Salt and pepper to taste

2/3 cup mango or peach chutney

1 to 2 tablespoons mild curry paste concentrate for sauces

1. Preheat the broiler. Line the broiler pan with aluminum foil. Spray the broiler pan rack with nonstick cooking spray. Trim any excess fat from the pork chops and place on the prepared broiler-pan rack. Season with salt and pepper.

2. If the pieces of fruit in the chutney are large, chop them with scissors or a knife. Place the chutney in a small bowl and add 1 to 2 tablespoons curry paste concentrate, beginning with about 1 tablespoon and adding more to taste. Spoon half of the sauce over the chops, spreading it to the edges.

3. Broil the chops 4 to 6 inches from the heat for 4 minutes for the thin chops; about 6 minutes for the thicker chops. Turn, spread the chops with the remaining chutney sauce, and broil for 5 to 7 minutes longer, depending upon thickness, or until the chops are no longer pink inside but still moist. Transfer to a serving platter, arranging the chops on one side.

step 3

assemble the **tomato and cucumber salad**

1/2 pint red globe or cherry tomatoes

1 bag (5 ounces) baby spinach leaves

10 ounces cucumber salad

2 tablespoons store-bought ranch salad dressing

Salt and pepper to taste

1. Rinse the tomatoes and pat dry.

2. Place the spinach in a shallow salad bowl. Add the tomatoes and cucumber salad. Add the dressing and salt and pepper and toss. Place the bowl on the table.

step 4

serve

1. Fluff the rice with a fork, add the chopped cashews, and toss. Mound the rice alongside the chops on the serving platter. Place the platter on the table.

2. When ready for dessert, divide the iced watermelon among 4 bowls. Plate the meringues and serve at once with the watermelon.

Broiled Pork Chops with Curried Chutney Sauce
Single serving is 1/4 of total recipe
CALORIES 290; PROTEIN 33g; CARBS 19g; TOTAL FAT 9g; SAT FAT 3g; CHOLESTEROL 92mg; SODIUM 306mg; FIBER 1g

☆ braised pork
with bacon and onions
quick polenta
tomatoes and basil on romaine
chilled green grapes and almond biscotti

menu
gameplan

shopping list

Bacon

Pork tenderloin

Pre-chopped garlic

Precooked ready-to-heat polenta

Ripe tomatoes

Fresh basil leaves

Balsamic vinaigrette dressing

Almond biscotti

from the salad bar

Onion slices

Torn romaine lettuce

Seedless green grapes (or from the produce department)

from your pantry

Olive oil

Fat-free reduced-sodium chicken broth

Dry white wine (optional)

Red wine vinegar

Bay leaves

Dried rosemary

Ground cloves

Salt and pepper

serves 4

beforeyoustart

Rinse the grapes and chill until serving time.

step 1 cook the **braised pork with bacon and onions**

step 2 prepare the **quick polenta**

step 3 assemble the **tomatoes and basil on romaine**

step 4 **serve**

luckyforyou
The sauce here is light and goes well with polenta, or with a broad pasta, such as pappardelle, or little Swiss-style spaetzle dumplings, or your favorite noodles.

"This comforting pork dish is inspired by a classic one of Northern Italy, where polenta is an alternative to rice, pasta, or bread."

—minutemeals' Chef Ruth

step 1

cook the **braised pork with bacon and onions**

4 slices bacon

1½ pounds pork tenderloin

2 tablespoons olive oil

1½ cups sliced onions

2 teaspoons pre-chopped garlic

1 cup fat-free reduced-sodium chicken broth

¼ cup dry white wine (or omit wine and use a total of 1¼ cups chicken broth)

1 tablespoon red wine vinegar

2 bay leaves

½ teaspoon crumbled dried rosemary

Pinch ground cloves

Salt and pepper

1. Slice the bacon crosswise into ½-inch strips. In a large heavy skillet or Dutch oven, cook the bacon over medium heat until crisp. Meanwhile, cut the pork tenderloin into 1-inch chunks. Remove the bacon with a slotted spoon and drain on paper towels; reserve.

2. Add the pork and 1 tablespoon of the olive oil to the skillet and cook over high heat, turning, just until no longer pink, about 3 minutes. Transfer to a plate.

3. Add the remaining 1 tablespoon olive oil, onions, and garlic to the skillet and cook, stirring occasionally, until the onions start to turn golden brown, about 3 minutes. Stir in the chicken broth, wine (if using), vinegar, bay leaves, rosemary, and a pinch of cloves. Cover and bring to a boil. Add the pork and any juices that have accumulated on the plate. Reduce the heat to medium-low, cover, and cook for 3 minutes, or until the pork is just tender.

step 2

prepare the **quick polenta**

1 package (about 16 ounces) precooked ready-to-heat polenta

Cut the roll of polenta into ½-inch-thick slices. Heat in the microwave, in a skillet, or in the oven according to the directions on the package.

step 3

assemble the **tomatoes and basil on romaine**

4 cups torn romaine lettuce

2 large or 3 medium ripe tomatoes

⅓ cup shredded fresh basil leaves

2 to 3 tablespoons balsamic vinaigrette dressing

1. Arrange about 1 cup of the romaine lettuce on each of 4 salad plates.

2. Rinse the tomatoes, pat dry, and thinly slice. Divide the slices among the salads.

3. Rinse the basil leaves, pat dry, and cut enough into shreds to measure ⅓ cup. Sprinkle over the tomatoes. Drizzle each salad with dressing. Place the salads on the table.

step 4

serve

1. Remove the bay leaves from the pork and stir in the reserved bacon. Season with salt and pepper.

2. Divide the slices of polenta among 4 large-rimmed soup bowls or pasta bowls and spoon the pork and sauce over them, dividing it equally. Serve, with the salads as an accompaniment.

3. When ready for dessert, place the grapes on a platter and surround with the biscotti. Serve as is or with 4 dessert plates.

Braised Pork with Bacon and Onions
Single serving is ¼ of total recipe

CALORIES 402; PROTEIN 43g; CARBS 5g; TOTAL FAT 22g; SAT FAT 6g; CHOLESTEROL 117mg; SODIUM 539mg; FIBER 1g

☆ sweet-and-sour pork

with peppers

pineapple rice

oranges and almond cookies

menu gameplan

shopping list

Instant brown rice

Juice-packed canned crushed pineapple

Pork tenderloin

Red pepper

Green pepper

Chinese duck sauce

Chopped scallions (from the salad bar)

Oranges

Chinese almond cookies (from the bakery)

from your pantry

Fat-free reduced-sodium chicken broth

Peanut or light olive oil

Ketchup

Cider or white vinegar

Lite soy sauce

serves 4

beforeyoustart

Bring water to a boil, covered, in a medium saucepan for the rice.

step 1   make the **pineapple rice**

step 2   cook the **sweet-and-sour pork with peppers**

step 3   **serve**

luckyforyou   Duck sauce, that sweet condiment that comes with most Chinese food, is readily available in the supermarket. If you're in a pinch, you can substitute an equal amount of apricot jam.

"You'll whip up this favorite in record time. Using brown rice, lean pork, and little oil makes this meal as healthy as it is delicious."

—minutemeals' Chef Paul

step 1

make the **pineapple rice**

2 cups instant brown rice

Fat-free reduced-sodium chicken broth

1/2 cup juice-packed canned crushed pineapple

1. Cook the brown rice according to the directions on the package, substituting chicken broth for the water.

2. Meanwhile, drain the pineapple. When the rice is done, add the pineapple to it, stirring to combine. Cover until serving time.

step 2

cook the **sweet-and-sour pork with peppers**

1 1/4 pounds pork tenderloin

1 medium-large red pepper

1 medium-large green pepper

2 tablespoons peanut or light olive oil

3/4 cup Chinese duck sauce

1 tablespoon ketchup

1 tablespoon cider or white vinegar

1 tablespoon lite soy sauce

1/2 cup chopped scallions

1. Cut the pork tenderloin into 1-inch chunks. Cut both peppers into 3/4-inch squares.

2. Heat 1 tablespoon of the oil in a large deep nonstick skillet over high heat until hot but not smoking. Add half the pork and cook, stirring occasionally, for 2 minutes, until no longer pink and lightly browned in spots. With a slotted spoon, transfer the pork to a bowl. Repeat with the remaining oil and pork.

3. Add the peppers to the pan juices in the skillet and toss. Reduce the heat to medium and cook, stirring occasionally, for 3 minutes, until crisp-tender.

4. Stir in the duck sauce, ketchup, vinegar, and soy sauce. Add the pork and any juices that have accumulated in the bowl and the scallions. Cook, stirring, for 1 to 2 minutes, or until the pork is no longer pink in the thickest part, but still juicy. Remove from the heat.

step 3

serve

1. Divide the rice among 4 serving bowls, top with pork stir-fry, and serve. Or, serve the rice on plates and place the stir-fry alongside.

2. When ready for dessert, cut the oranges into wedges, place the wedges on a plate, and serve with the almond cookies.

Sweet-and-Sour Pork with Peppers
Single serving is 1/4 of total recipe

CALORIES 331; PROTEIN 31g; CARBS 24g; TOTAL FAT 12g; SAT FAT 3g; CHOLESTEROL 84mg; SODIUM 406mg; FIBER 2g

molasses and black pepper pork tenderloin

sour cream mashed potatoes

buttered green beans

blondies

shopping list

Cracked black pepper

Pork tenderloins

Small thin-skinned new potatoes

Light sour cream

Pretrimmed green beans or frozen cut green beans

Blondies (from the bakery)

from your pantry

Canola oil

Molasses

Ground cumin

Coarse salt

Butter

Salt and pepper

serves 4

beforeyoustart

Preheat the oven to 425°F to roast the pork.

| step | 1 | roast the **molasses and black pepper pork tenderloin** |

| step | 2 | cook the **sour cream mashed potatoes** |

| step | 3 | cook the **buttered green beans** |

| step | 4 | serve |

headsup

Although the brief cooking time needed by the pork tenderloin is a boon to busy cooks, it is also not quite enough to impart a crispy, brown exterior to the meat. The molasses helps a bit. Here is something else you can do. Try lightly browning the tenderloins first in a hot pan filmed with canola oil.

"This is a meat-and-potatoes menu—simple but good for family or friends. Dress up the dessert, if you like, for company."

—minutemeals' Chef Marge

step 1

roast the **molasses and black pepper pork tenderloin**

1¹/₂ tablespoons canola oil

2 tablespoons molasses

1 tablespoon cracked black pepper

1 teaspoon ground cumin

1 teaspoon coarse salt

1 package pork tenderloin (2 pieces, about 1³/₄ pounds total weight)

1. Preheat the oven to 425°F. Coat a roasting pan or the bottom of the broiler pan with 1 tablespoon of the canola oil. Place in oven to heat for 2 minutes.

2. In a small bowl, combine the molasses, pepper, cumin, and salt. Rub the mixture over the pork tenderloins.

3. Place the tenderloins on the hot pan. Drizzle with the remaining ¹/₂ tablespoon oil. Roast in the center of the oven until a meat thermometer registers 155°F, 12 to 15 minutes. Remove the tenderloins to a cutting board.

step 2

cook the **sour cream mashed potatoes**

1¹/₂ pounds small thin-skinned potatoes

2 tablespoons butter

¹/₃ cup light sour cream

Salt and pepper to taste

1. Scrub the potatoes and cut them in half. Place in a medium saucepan. Add cold water just to cover, cover the pan, and bring to a boil over high heat. Reduce the heat to medium, cover partially, and simmer 8 to 10 minutes, or until the potatoes are tender when pierced with a knife. Reserve about 1 cup of the cooking water and drain.

2. Add the butter and sour cream to the pan, top with the potatoes, and mash to a coarse texture with a potato masher. Add enough of the reserved cooking water (about ¹/₂ cup) for a creamy consistency. Season with salt and pepper. Keep warm, covered.

step 3

cook the **buttered green beans**

1 pound pretrimmed fresh or cut frozen green beans

Salt to taste

1 tablespoon butter

1. Fill a large skillet with 1 inch water, cover and bring to a boil over high heat. Add a pinch of salt and the beans. Cover the pan, reduce the heat slightly, and simmer for 4 to 6 minutes, until tender. (Cook frozen beans according to the directions on the package.)

2. Drain fresh or frozen beans and transfer to a serving dish. Add the butter and salt to taste. Toss to melt the butter and place the dish on the table.

step 4

serve

1. Slice the tenderloins into thin medallions and divide them among 4 dinner plates.

2. Add a serving of mashed potatoes to each plate and serve with the green beans as an accompaniment.

3. When ready for dessert, serve the blondies on a small platter.

Molasses and Black Pepper Pork Tenderloin
Single serving is ¹/₄ of total recipe
CALORIES 323; PROTEIN 42g; CARBS 8g; TOTAL FAT 12g; SAT FAT 3g; CHOLESTEROL 118mg; SODIUM 559mg; FIBER 1g

green chili stew
cheese and corn tortillas
tropical fruit cups

shopping list

Cilantro

Pork for stir-fry

Canned white beans, such as navy or cannellini beans

Green salsa

Reduced-fat sour cream

Ripe bananas

Cubed pineapple (from the salad bar) or juice-packed canned pineapple

Dulce de leche frozen yogurt or ice cream

Corn tortillas (6-inch diameter)

Pre-shredded Monterey Jack cheese

Frozen or canned corn kernels

from your pantry

Onion

Olive oil

Fat-free reduced-sodium chicken broth

Ground cumin

Salt and pepper

Sugar

Rum (or orange juice)

Chili powder

serves 4

beforeyoustart
Preheat the oven to 425°F to bake the tortillas.

step **1** cook the **green chili stew**

step **2** while the chili is cooking, assemble the **tropical fruit cups**

step **3** bake the **cheese and corn tortillas**

step **4** **serve**

headsup For a thicker chili, don't add more beans or meat. Just mash some of the beans against the side of the pot. Want red chili? Use red salsa.

"Sliced pork and jarred salsa make this the quickest-cooking chili around. Cilantro brightens the flavor and sour cream tames the heat."

—minutemeals' Chef Sarah

step 1

cook the **green chili stew**

1/4 cup chopped cilantro

1 small onion

1 pound pork for stir-fry

2 cans (15 ounces each) white beans such as navy or cannellini beans

1 tablespoon olive oil

1 can (14 1/2 ounces) fat-free reduced-sodium chicken broth

1 jar (16 ounces) prepared green salsa

1 1/2 teaspoons ground cumin

Salt and pepper to taste

1/2 cup reduced-fat sour cream

1. Chop enough cilantro to measure 1/4 cup. Finely chop the onion. Cut the pork strips into 1-inch pieces. Rinse and drain the beans.

2. In a 6-quart pot, heat the olive oil over high heat until hot. Add the onion and pork and cook, stirring frequently, until the pork browns, about 3 minutes.

3. Stir in the white beans, chicken broth, salsa, and cumin and season with salt and pepper. Cover and bring to a boil over medium-high heat. Remove the cover, reduce the heat to medium, and simmer, stirring occasionally, for 8 minutes.

step 2

assemble the **tropical fruit cups**

2 large ripe bananas

2 cups cubed fresh pineapple or drained juice-packed canned pineapple

2 tablespoons sugar

2 tablespoons rum or orange juice

4 small scoops dulce de leche frozen yogurt or ice cream

1. Peel and slice the bananas into a medium bowl.

2. Add the pineapple, sugar, and rum. Toss to combine. Refrigerate until serving time.

step 3

bake the **cheese and corn tortillas**

4 corn tortillas (6-inch diameter)

3/4 cup pre-shredded Monterey Jack cheese

1/2 cup frozen or drained canned corn kernels

1/2 teaspoon chili powder

1. Preheat the oven to 425°F. Place the tortillas on a cookie sheet.

2. In a small bowl, stir together the cheese, corn, and chili powder. Spread the mixture on the tortillas. Bake for 6 to 8 minutes, until the tortillas are crisp and the cheese is bubbly. Cut into wedges, and serve warm.

step 4

serve

1. Stir the cilantro into the chili. Ladle the chili into 4 soup or pasta bowls and garnish with spoonfuls of sour cream. Serve with the tortilla wedges on the side.

2. When ready for dessert, spoon the frozen yogurt or ice cream into 4 small dessert bowls and top with the mixed fruit. Serve.

Green Chili Stew
Single serving is 1/4 of total recipe

CALORIES 402; PROTEIN 35g; CARBS 35g; TOTAL FAT 16g; SAT FAT 6g; CHOLESTEROL 84mg; SODIUM 1451mg; FIBER 10g

☆ asian pork and noodles

radish and cucumber salad
tapioca parfaits

menu
gameplan

shopping list

Fresh pineapple rings (from the produce department) or juice-packed canned pineapple

Ready-to-serve tapioca pudding

Watercress or prewashed mixed salad greens

Red wine vinegar and oil salad dressing

Lite coconut milk

Thai yellow curry paste

Chicken-flavored ramen noodle soup

Red pepper

Unsalted peanuts

Pork for stir-fry

Lime (optional)

from the salad bar

Radish slices

Cucumber slices

Chopped scallions

from your pantry

Honey

Salt and pepper

Vegetable oil

serves 4

beforeyoustart

Bring 2 cups of water to a boil in a large pot, covered, over high heat to cook the noodles.

step	1	assemble the **tapioca parfaits**
step	2	assemble the **radish and cucumber salad**
step	3	cook the **asian pork and noodles**
step	4	**serve**

heads up
Thai curry paste is available in the Asiatic foods sections of many supermarkets. The pastes can have varying degrees of heat. If you cannot find the yellow paste that's called for here, use green or red curry paste instead.

"This easy but exotic combination of noodles, pork, and vegetables with coconut milk tastes as if it took hours to prepare. It's great with chicken, too."

—minutemeals' Chef Sarah

step 1

assemble the **tapioca parfaits**

4 rings peeled fresh pineapple or drained juice-packed canned pineapple

2 tablespoons honey

1 container (22 ounces) refrigerated ready-to-serve tapioca pudding

1. Dice the pineapple.

2. In a medium bowl, combine the pineapple and honey.

3. In 4 parfait glasses, alternately layer pudding and pineapple. Refrigerate the parfaits until serving time.

step 2

assemble the **radish and cucumber salad**

1 bunch watercress, stems trimmed, rinsed, and spun dry; or 2 cups prewashed mixed salad greens

1/2 cup radish slices

1/2 cup cucumber slices

2 tablespoons store-bought red wine vinegar and oil salad dressing

Salt and pepper to taste

1. Stem, rinse, and spin dry the watercress.

2. In a medium bowl, combine the radishes, cucumber slices, and salad dressing, and season with salt and pepper. Top with the watercress or mixed greens; do not toss until serving time. Place the bowl on the table with 4 salad plates.

step 3

cook the **asian pork and noodles**

2 cups water

1 can (14 ounces) lite coconut milk

3 teaspoons Thai yellow curry paste (or powder)

2 packages (3 ounces each) chicken-flavored ramen noodle soup

1 large red pepper

1/3 cup unsalted peanuts

1 tablespoon vegetable oil

1 pound pork for stir-fry

1 cup chopped scallions

Lime wedges (optional)

1. Pour the water into a large pot or Dutch oven, cover, and bring to a boil over high heat. Add the coconut milk, 2 teaspoons of the yellow curry paste, and the seasoning packets from the soup mixes. Stir; reduce the heat slightly, and boil for 3 minutes. Add the noodles and cook, stirring frequently, for 2 minutes, or until the noodles soften. Cover and remove the pan from the heat.

2. Thinly slice the red pepper. Chop the peanuts and reserve.

3. In a large nonstick skillet, heat the vegetable oil and remaining 1 teaspoon curry paste over high heat, stirring to blend. Add the pork and stir-fry for 1 minute. Add the pepper slices and stir-fry for 2 to 3 minutes, until the pork is cooked through and the peppers are slightly tender. Stir in the scallions.

step 4

serve

1. Divide the noodles and sauce among 4 soup or pasta bowls. Top with the pork stir-fry. Sprinkle chopped peanuts over each bowl, garnish each with a lime wedge, if desired, and serve.

2. Toss the salad at the table, and serve it on the salad plates.

3. When ready for dessert, serve the parfaits.

Asian Pork and Noodles
Single serving is 1/4 of total recipe
CALORIES 569; PROTEIN 32g; CARBS 37g; TOTAL FAT 32g; SAT FAT 14g; CHOLESTEROL 68mg; SODIUM 853mg; FIBER 4g

greek souvlaki
on pita bread
feta-olive salad
frozen fruit pops

serves 4

beforeyoustart
Preheat the oven to 350°F to heat the pita breads.

| step | 1 | assemble the **feta-olive salad** |

| step | 2 | make the **greek souvlaki on pita bread** |

| step | 3 | **serve** |

shopping list

Italian salad dressing

Kalamata olives, pitted

Crumbled feta cheese

Prewashed colorful crisp salad greens

Pita breads (6-inch diameter)

Fresh mint

Cucumber slices (from the salad bar)

Tomato

Pork for stir-fry

Plain low-fat yogurt

Frozen fruit Pops

from your pantry

Garlic

Salt and pepper

 Feta cheese is now available crumbled and even flavored.

"Greek food is popular and as you can see from this easy menu, you don't have to go to a special restaurant to have it."

—minutemeals' Chef Sarah

step 1

assemble the **feta-olive salad**

3 tablespoons store-bought Italian salad dressing

1/2 cup pitted kalamata olives

1/3 cup crumbled feta cheese

1 bag (10 ounces) prewashed colorful crisp salad greens

In a large bowl, combine the dressing, olives, and feta. Top with the salad greens. Place the bowl on the table.

step 2

make the **greek souvlaki on pita bread**

4 pita breads (6-inch diameter)

3/4 teaspoon minced garlic (1 garlic clove)

3 tablespoons chopped fresh mint

3/4 cup cucumber slices

1 medium tomato

2 tablespoons store-bought Italian salad dressing

3/4 pound pork for stir-fry

Salt and pepper to taste

1/2 cup plain low-fat yogurt for serving

1. Preheat the oven to 350°F.

2. Wrap the pita breads in aluminum foil. Place in the oven to warm.

3. Mince the garlic. Chop enough mint to measure 3 tablespoons. Stack cucumber slices and cut into thin matchsticks. Rinse the tomato, pat dry, and coarsely chop. Put the cucumber and tomato in separate bowls.

4. In a medium bowl, combine 1/2 teaspoon minced garlic, 1 tablespoon Italian dressing, and the pork. Season with salt and pepper and toss to coat.

5. In another small bowl, stir together the remaining 1/4 teaspoon garlic, the chopped mint, salt and pepper, and the yogurt.

6. In a large nonstick skillet, heat the remaining 1 tablespoon salad dressing over medium-high heat. Add the pork and stir-fry it until lightly browned and cooked through, 3 to 4 minutes. Remove the pan from the heat. Transfer the pork to a serving bowl.

step 3

serve

1. Place the pork, cucumbers, tomatoes, yogurt sauce, and pitas on the table. Instead of filling the pita pockets, spoon the filling in the center of each of the breads, then fold in the sides and eat like a taco.

2. Toss the salad and serve as an accompaniment to the souvlaki.

3. When ready for dessert, serve the fruit Pops directly from the freezer.

Greek Souvlaki on Pita Bread
Single serving is 1/4 of total recipe

CALORIES 363; PROTEIN 26g; CARBS 39g; TOTAL FAT 11g; SAT FAT 3g; CHOLESTEROL 53mg; SODIUM 583mg; FIBER 2g

☆ braised lamb chops
with spring vegetables
quick rice
waffles suzette

shopping list

Blade or round bone
shoulder lamb chops

Baby carrots

Frozen baby peas

Toaster waffles

Vanilla frozen yogurt

from your pantry

Salt and pepper

Olive oil

All-purpose flour

Fat-free reduced-sodium
beef broth

Dry red wine

Garlic

Dried rosemary

Instant rice

Fat-free reduced-sodium
chicken broth (optional)

Butter

Sugar

Orange juice

Grand Marnier

menu
gameplan

serves 4

step **1** cook the **braised lamb chops with spring vegetables**

step **2** prepare the **quick rice**

step **3** prepare the **waffles suzette**

step **4** serve

 The braising liquid is the sauce for the chops. In other words, no reduction or additional cooking of a sauce is necessary. Serve as is.

"Lamb with fresh spring vegetables is a classic French combination, especially in the spring, but you can have this simplified version year round."

—minutemeals' Chef Hillary

step 1

cook the **braised lamb chops with spring vegetables**

4 blade or round bone shoulder lamb chops (about 6 ounces each)

Salt and pepper to taste

1 tablespoon olive oil

3 tablespoons all-purpose flour

1 can (14^1/2 ounces) fat-free reduced-sodium beef broth

3 tablespoons dry red wine

2 garlic cloves

1^1/2 teaspoons crumbled dried rosemary

1^1/2 cups baby carrots

1 package (10 ounces) frozen baby peas

1. Trim the lamb chops. Season with salt and pepper.

2. In a large deep heavy skillet, heat the olive oil over high heat. Add the lamb chops and cook for 3 to 5 minutes on each side, or until nicely browned. Transfer to a platter.

3. Add the flour to the pan drippings. Cook, stirring rapidly with a wooden spoon, about 1 minute or until the flour starts to brown but isn't scorched.

4. Using a wire whisk, slowly add the broth and wine until the flour mixture is well incorporated.

Crush the garlic in a garlic press. Add the garlic and the rosemary to the skillet and bring to a boil, whisking. Reduce to a simmer; add the lamb chops with any juices that have accumulated on the plate. Cover the pan and simmer for 5 minutes.

5. Turn the lamb in the sauce and add the vegetables. Cover and cook for 5 to 7 minutes, until the lamb and vegetables are tender.

step 2

prepare the **quick rice**

2 cups instant rice

4 cups water or fat-free reduced-sodium chicken broth

Prepare the rice in a medium saucepan with the water or chicken broth according to the directions on the package.

step 3

prepare the **waffles suzette**

4 tablespoons butter

2 tablespoons sugar

^{1}/2 cup orange juice

2 tablespoons Grand Marnier or orange-flavored liqueur

4 toaster waffles

Vanilla frozen yogurt

1. Place the butter and the sugar in a large deep nonstick skillet and cook over medium-high heat until the butter melts. Stir in the orange juice and Grand Marnier, cover and bring to a boil. Reduce to ^{1}/2 cup.

2. Toast the waffles according to the directions on the package. Place 1 on each of 4 dessert plates.

step 4

serve

1. Divide the rice among 4 dinner plates.

2. Top each serving of rice with a lamb chop and some of the vegetables and sauce. Serve at once.

3. When ready for dessert, spoon suzette sauce over each waffle, then top with a scoop of frozen yogurt. Serve.

Braised Lamb Chops with Spring Vegetables
Single serving is ^{1}/4 of total recipe
CALORIES 377; PROTEIN 37g; CARBS 21g; TOTAL FAT 16g; SAT FAT 5g; CHOLESTEROL 101mg; SODIUM 358mg; FIBER 5g

meat menus • 89

lamb chops
with garlic and mint sauce

micro-baked new potatoes
broiled tomatoes with garlic crumbs
raspberry and cream sorbet

menu gameplan

shopping list

Thin-skinned potatoes

Blade or round bone shoulder lamb chops

Fresh mint

Tomatoes

Raspberry and cream sorbet

from your pantry

Butter or reduced-fat sour cream

Salt and pepper

Garlic

Sugar

Red wine or balsamic vinegar

Seasoned dry bread crumbs

Olive oil

Herb-and-garlic seasoning

serves 4

beforeyoustart
Preheat the broiler.

step **1** cook the **micro-baked new potatoes**

step **2** broil the **lamb chops with garlic and mint sauce**

step **3** make the broiled **tomatoes with garlic crumbs**

step **4** **serve**

luckyforyou Make the garlic and mint sauce ahead of time. The longer it stands, the better the flavor.

"Make sure you serve this menu to garlic lovers. There's a lot of garlic here. Why? Because lamb with garlic is so good."

—minutemeals' Chef Hillary

step 1

cook the **micro-baked new potatoes**

1¼ pounds medium thin-skinned potatoes

Butter or reduced-fat sour cream for serving

Salt and pepper for serving

1. Scrub the potatoes and pierce each one several times with a skewer or fork.

2. Place the potatoes in the microwave oven and microwave on High, turning them over halfway through cooking, about 4 to 6 minutes, until tender. Remove from the oven and let stand before serving.

step 2

broil the **lamb chops with garlic and mint sauce**

2 large garlic cloves

8 blade or round bone shoulder lamb chops (about 6 ounces each)

Salt and pepper to taste

¼ cup sugar

2 tablespoons water

2 tablespoons red wine or balsamic vinegar

2 tablespoons chopped fresh mint leaves

1. Preheat the broiler. Line the broiler pan with aluminum foil.

2. Cut 1 of the garlic cloves in half; chop the remaining garlic clove.

3. Trim the lamb chops. Rub the chops with the cut sides of the garlic. Season the chops with salt and pepper. Place the chops on the prepared broiler-pan rack. Broil 4 to 5 inches from the heat for 4 to 6 minutes per side for medium. Transfer the chops to a platter and cover loosely with foil to keep warm. Do not turn off the broiler.

4. Meanwhile, in a small saucepan, stir together the sugar and water. Bring to a boil over high heat and boil for 2 minutes. Remove from the heat and stir in the chopped garlic and vinegar. Let cool slightly.

5. Chop enough fresh mint to measure 2 tablespoons and stir it into the sauce. Keep warm, partially covered.

step 3

make the **broiled tomatoes with garlic crumbs**

2 large tomatoes

½ cup seasoned dry bread crumbs

2 tablespoons olive oil

½ teaspoon herb-and-garlic seasoning

1. Line a jelly-roll pan with aluminum foil.

2. Rinse the tomatoes, pat dry, and cut into thick slices.

3. In a small bowl, stir together the bread crumbs, olive oil, and herb-and-garlic seasoning. Spoon the crumb mixture onto each tomato slice. Broil for 3 to 4 minutes, or until heated and the crumbs are lightly browned.

step 4

serve

1. Transfer the potatoes to a serving bowl and place on the table with butter or sour cream and salt and pepper for serving.

2. Place a lamb chop on each of 4 dinner plates and add a serving of the tomatoes to each. Serve.

3. Pour the garlic and mint sauce into a small bowl and pass as an accompaniment, to be added by each diner, to the lamb chops.

4. When ready for dessert, scoop the sorbet into 4 dessert bowls and serve.

Lamb Chops with Garlic and Mint Sauce
Single serving is ¼ of total recipe

CALORIES 497; PROTEIN 54g; CARBS 13g; TOTAL FAT 24g; SAT FAT 9g; CHOLESTEROL 193mg; SODIUM 334mg; FIBER 0g

rib lamb chops
with scallion crust

new potatoes with olive oil and lemon

buttery peas with wilted spinach

lemon-lime sherbet with wafer cookies

menu gameplan

shopping list

New potatoes

Lemon (for juice)

Scallions

Rib lamb chops

Baby spinach

Frozen petite peas

Lemon-lime sherbet

Wafer cookies

from your pantry

Salt

Extra virgin olive oil

Freshly ground black pepper

Extra-thin white bread

Garlic

Dried rosemary

Butter

Dried tarragon or thyme

serves 4

beforeyou**start**

Preheat the oven to 475°F to cook the lamb chops.

step **1** cook the **new potatoes with olive oil and lemon**

step **2** cook the **rib lamb chops with scallion crust**

step **3** cook the **buttery peas with wilted spinach**

step **4** **serve**

luckyforyou You don't need a food processor to make fresh bread crumbs here. Just dice 3 slices of extra-thin white bread very fine.

"Rack of lamb is a special cut of meat. This recipe is reminiscent of a rack, only much simpler. It is also elegant, ideal for company."

—minutemeals' Chef Hillary

step 1

cook the **new potatoes with olive oil and lemon**

1½ pounds tiny new potatoes

Salt to taste

2 teaspoons extra virgin olive oil

2 teaspoons fresh lemon juice

Freshly ground black pepper to taste

1. Halve the potatoes. Put the potatoes in a medium saucepan and add ½ inch cold water and salt to taste. Cover and bring to a boil over high heat. Reduce the heat to medium and cook, partially covered, for 6 minutes, or until tender when tested with a fork.

2. Drain the potatoes, transfer to a serving bowl, and drizzle with the olive oil and lemon juice. Season with fresh pepper and toss gently. Place the bowl on the table.

step 2

cook the **rib lamb chops with scallion crust**

1 bunch of scallions

3 slices extra-thin white bread

2 garlic cloves

2 tablespoons extra virgin olive oil

2 teaspoons dried rosemary

Salt and pepper to taste

8 rib lamb chops (2 to 3 ounces each)

1. Preheat the oven to 475°F.

2. Thinly slice the scallions. Finely chop enough bread to measure 1 cup of bread crumbs. Crush the garlic in a garlic press.

3. In a small nonstick skillet, heat the olive oil over medium heat. Add the scallions, garlic, and rosemary and cook for 2 minutes, or until the scallions have wilted. Stir in the bread crumbs and season with salt and pepper. Remove from the heat.

4. Heat 2 large ovenproof skillets over high heat. Season the lamb chops with salt and pepper. Place 4 chops in each skillet and cook for 3 minutes, until browned on the underside. Turn and top the meaty part of each chop with about 1 tablespoon of the scallion mixture. Place the skillets in the oven to bake for 5 minutes for medium-rare.

Note: If you do not have 2 large ovenproof skillets, use 1 skillet to brown the chops in batches on one side. Turn and place the chops, uncooked side up, on a jelly-roll or roasting pan. Spoon the crumb mixture on top and place the pan in the oven as directed.

step 3

cook the **buttery peas with wilted spinach**

2 tablespoons butter

¼ teaspoon crumbled dried tarragon or thyme

1 bag (5 ounces) baby spinach

1 package (10 ounces) frozen petite peas

2 tablespoons water

Salt and pepper to taste

1. Melt the butter in a large deep nonstick skillet over medium-high heat. Add the tarragon or thyme and the spinach (in batches, if necessary). Cook, tossing, until the spinach just wilts, about 1 minute.

2. Add the peas and water. Reduce the heat to medium. Cover and cook, stirring once or twice, for 3 minutes, until the peas are heated. Season with salt and pepper. Transfer to a serving bowl and place the bowl on the table.

step 4

serve

1. Trying not to dislodge the scallion crust, transfer 2 lamb chops to each of 4 dinner plates. Serve at once with the potatoes and peas.

2. When ready for dessert, scoop the sorbet into 4 dessert cups and garnish each with 1 or 2 wafer cookies. Serve.

Rib Lamb Chops with Scallion Crust
Single serving is ¼ of total recipe
CALORIES 297; PROTEIN 12g; CARBS 8g; TOTAL FAT 24g; SAT FAT 9g; CHOLESTEROL 57mg; SODIUM 231mg; FIBER 1g

minute
3 ways

chapter 3

seafood menus

micro-poached salmon
with summery salsa
potato salad
crisp sesame flatbreads
toasted pound cake with strawberries

serves 4

shopping list

Vacuum-packed canned corn kernels

Yellow or red pepper

Fresh parsley

Mild salsa, refrigerated or jarred

Salmon fillet pieces

Fresh dill or scallions

Prepared potato salad (from the deli counter or prepared foods section)

Plain or marble pound cake

Frozen strawberries packed in lite syrup

Crisp sesame flatbreads

from your pantry

Olive oil

Salt and pepper

Hot pepper sauce

Dry white wine or fresh lemon juice

Confectioners' sugar

beforeyoustart

Thaw the frozen strawberries for dessert.

step	1	prepare the **summery salsa**
step	2	prepare the **micro-poached salmon**
step	3	plate the **potato salad**
step	4	prepare the **toasted pound cake with strawberries**
step	5	**serve**

 luckyforyou The microwave oven makes quick work of this menu. If you don't own a microwave, poach the salmon in a tightly covered heavy nonstick skillet on the range-top over very low heat, simmering gently, until the fish tests done. Depending on the size of your skillet, you may need to use 2 pans.

"Cook an extra fillet or two, chill, and serve them the next day with mayonnaise laced with minced garlic. That's 2 meals in 20 minutes!"

—minutemeals' Chef Ruth

step 1
prepare the **summery salsa**

1 can (12 ounces) drained vacuum-packed corn kernels

1/2 cup chopped yellow or red pepper (1 medium pepper)

2 tablespoons chopped parsley

1/2 cup prepared mild salsa

1 tablespoon olive oil

Salt and pepper to taste

1/8 to 1/4 teaspoon hot pepper sauce

1. Drain the corn. Chop enough of the yellow or red pepper to measure 1/2 cup. Chop enough parsley to measure 2 tablespoons.

2. In a medium bowl, stir together the corn, chopped pepper, parsley, salsa, and olive oil. Season with salt and pepper. Stir in the hot pepper sauce to taste. Cover and refrigerate until serving time.

step 2
prepare the **micro-poached salmon**

4 pieces of salmon fillet (5 to 6 ounces each)

Salt and pepper to taste

Several large sprigs of fresh dill or 4 scallions

1/3 cup dry white wine or use 1/4 cup water and 1 tablespoon fresh lemon juice

1. Rinse the salmon fillets and pat dry with paper towels.

2. Arrange the salmon, skin side down, in a microwave-safe dish 1 to 2 inches deep, just large enough to hold the fillets without overlapping. Place the thicker sections of the fillets toward the outside edge of the dish. Season with salt and pepper. Place the dill sprigs over the salmon or place a trimmed scallion on each fillet. Pour the wine or water and lemon juice combination over the salmon. Cover the dish with a lid or vented microwave-safe plastic wrap. Microwave on High until the fish is no longer translucent but is still moist and flakes with a fork, 4 to 7 minutes, depending on the thickness, rotating the dish halfway through cooking. (Check every minute after 4 minutes.) Let stand 1 or 2 minutes before removing cover or plastic wrap.

step 3
plate the **potato salad**

prepared potato salad for 4

Spoon the potato salad into a serving bowl and place the bowl on the table.

step 4
prepare the **toasted pound cake with strawberries**

1 store-bought plain or marble pound cake

Confectioners' sugar for dusting

1 package (10 ounces) frozen strawberries in lite syrup

1. Preheat a toaster oven.

2. Cut the pound cake into 1-inch-thick slices and place on the pan of the toaster oven. Sprinkle with a thick dusting of confectioners' sugar. Broil 2 to 3 minutes, watching closely, until the slices are browned and crisp looking. Remove and let stand until serving time.

step 5
serve

1. With a broad spatula, remove the salmon pieces from the dish and place 1 piece on each dinner plate. Spoon the pan juices over the fish Spoon about 1/2 cup salsa alongside. Serve the salmon with the potato salad and flatbreads.

2. When ready for dessert, place a slice of toasted pound cake on each of 4 dessert plates. Spoon strawberries and syrup over each serving. Or place the berries and syrup in a serving bowl and pass at the table.

Micro-Poached Salmon with Summery Salsa
Single serving is 1/4 of total recipe

CALORIES 268; PROTEIN 29g; CARBS 20g; TOTAL FAT 9g; SAT FAT 1g; CHOLESTEROL 69mg; SODIUM 612mg; FIBER 3g

☆ baked salmon
with crunchy mustard crust

orzo with pesto
peas and carrots
mixed fruits with lemon sorbet

menu
gameplan

serves 4

shopping list

Cheese-garlic or plain croutons

Salmon fillet pieces

Orzo or other small pasta

Prepared pesto

Frozen peas and carrots

Mixed fruit salad (strawberries, pineapple, grapes, jarred in the produce department)

Lemon sorbet

from your pantry

Nonstick vegetable cooking spray

Grated Parmesan cheese

Regular or reduced-fat mayonnaise

Grainy mustard

Salt and pepper

beforeyoustart
Bring a saucepan of water, covered, to a boil to cook the orzo.

step **1** make the **baked salmon with crunchy mustard crust**

step **2** meanwhile, cook the **orzo with pesto**

step **3** cook the **peas and carrots**

step **4** prepare the **mixed fruits with lemon sorbet**

step **5** **serve**

luckyforyou
Either regular or reduced-fat mayonnaise works equally well in the salmon recipe. Avoid nonfat or imitation mayonnaise.

"There are health reasons to eat salmon and to eat it often. The challenge is to keep it interesting. The crunchy crust here does that."

—minutemeals' Chef Ruth

step 1

make the **baked salmon with crunchy mustard crust**

Nonstick vegetable cooking spray

About 1 cup cheese-garlic or plain croutons

2 tablespoons grated Parmesan cheese

1/3 cup regular or reduced-fat mayonnaise

1 tablespoon grainy mustard

4 pieces of salmon fillet (about 6 ounces each and uniformly thick as possible)

1. Spray a jelly-roll pan with nonstick vegetable cooking spray.

2. Crush the croutons in a blender or food processor to make about 2/3 cup rough-textured crumbs. (Or place the croutons in a plastic bag and crush with a mallet.) Transfer to a bowl and stir in the Parmesan.

3. In a small bowl, stir together the mayonnaise and mustard.

4. Rinse the salmon pieces and pat dry with paper towels. Place, skin side down, on the prepared pan. With a small spatula, spread the top of each with some of the mayonnaise mixture. Sprinkle the fillets with a thick coating of the crumb mixture, pressing down with the spatula to make the crumbs adhere. Bake in a 425° oven for 15 to 20 minutes, until crispy on the outside but still very moist within and just opaque and flakes when tested with a fork. (Time will vary with thickness of fillets.)

step 2

cook the **orzo with pesto**

2 quarts water

Salt to taste

1 cup (about 6 ounces) orzo or other small pasta

3 tablespoons prepared pesto sauce

Pepper to taste

1. Pour the water into a large saucepan, salt lightly, and cover. Bring to a boil over high heat. Add the orzo or pasta, stir to separate, and cook according to the directions on the package until *al dente*. Reserve 2 tablespoons of the pasta cooking water and drain well.

2. Transfer the orzo to a serving bowl and stir in the pesto and reserved cooking water until well combined. Season with salt and pepper. Place the bowl on the table.

step 3

cook the **peas and carrots**

1 bag (16 ounces) frozen peas and carrots

In a medium saucepan, cook the mixed vegetables according to the directions on the package. Drain, if necessary, and transfer to a serving bowl. Place the bowl on the table.

step 4

prepare the **mixed fruits with lemon sorbet**

1 quart mixed fruit salad (strawberries, pineapple, grapes)

1 pint lemon sorbet

1. Drain the fruit salad of most of its juice and place in a serving bowl.

2. Remove the sorbet from the freezer to soften before serving, if desired.

step 5

serve

1. With a wide spatula, place a piece of salmon on each of 4 dinner plates. Serve, with the orzo and peas and carrots as accompaniments.

2. When ready for dessert, spoon the fruit salad into 4 dessert bowls and top each with a small scoop of the sorbet. Serve.

Baked Salmon with Crunchy Mustard Crust
Single serving is 1/4 of total recipe

CALORIES 380; PROTEIN 34g; CARBS 7g; TOTAL FAT 23g; SAT FAT 4g; CHOLESTEROL 97mg; SODIUM 482mg; FIBER 1g

soy- and honey-glazed salmon
peanutty noodles
steamed broccoli
spice cake with sliced peaches

menu gameplan

shopping list

Packaged thin Chinese noodles

Bottled spicy peanut sauce

Broccoli florets (from the salad bar or produce department)

Salmon fillet pieces

Limes or lemon (for juice)

Spice cake (from the bakery or freezer section)

Sliced peaches

from your pantry

Salt and pepper

Toasted sesame oil

Lite soy sauce

Honey

Dijon mustard

Vegetable oil

serves 4

beforeyoustart

Bring a large pot of water to a boil, covered, over high heat to cook the noodles.

step 1 cook the **peanutty noodles**

step 2 prepare the **steamed broccoli**

step 3 cook the **soy- and honey-glazed salmon**

step 4 **serve**

luckyforyou Feel free to substitute rice noodles or plain rice for the flour-based noodles here. If using rice noodles or plain rice, omit the peanut sauce entirely, and simply serve the salmon on a bed of the noodles or rice.

"Use salmon steaks here, if you prefer. If thicker than $3/4$ inch, allow 4 to 5 minutes cooking per side, just until fish tests done."

—minutemeals' Chef Ruth

step 1

cook the **peanutty noodles**

3 quarts water

Salt to taste

4 ounces (about) packaged thin Chinese noodles

$1/3$ cup bottled spicy peanut sauce

1. Pour the water into a large saucepan, salt lightly, and cover. Bring to a boil over high heat. Add the noodles, stir to separate the strands, and cook according to the directions on the package. Drain well.

2. Place the noodles in a serving bowl and add the peanut sauce. Toss well to coat.

step 2

prepare the **steamed broccoli**

4 cups broccoli florets

Salt and pepper to taste

$1/2$ teaspoons toasted sesame oil

Pour $1/2$ cup water into a medium saucepan. Place the broccoli florets in a steamer basket and set the basket in the saucepan. Place the pan over high heat and steam until the broccoli is bright green and crisp-tender, about 5 to 7 minutes. Drain, place in a serving bowl, season with salt and pepper, and drizzle with the sesame oil. Keep warm, covered.

step 3

cook the **soy- and honey-glazed salmon**

4 pieces of salmon fillet, each $3/4$ inch thick (about $1^1/2$ pounds total weight)

3 tablespoons fresh lime or lemon juice (2 medium limes or 1 large lemon)

$1/4$ cup lite soy sauce

3 tablespoons honey

1 tablespoon Dijon mustard

2 teaspoons vegetable oil

1. Rinse the salmon and pat dry with paper towels.

2. Squeeze enough lime or lemon juice to measure 3 tablespoons. Place the juice in a small bowl and add the soy sauce, honey, and mustard. Whisk to blend.

3. Heat the vegetable oil in a large nonstick skillet over medium heat until hot but not smoking. Add the salmon pieces, skin side up, and cook for 3 minutes. Turn the pieces, pour the soy mixture into the skillet, and bring to a simmer. Cook, occasionally spooning glaze over the fillets, until the fish is just opaque but is still very moist, about 3 minutes more. (Time will vary with thickness of fillets.) Transfer the pieces to a serving platter.

4. Continue to simmer the glaze until it has a syrupy consistency. Spoon the glaze over the fillets.

step 4

serve

1. Divide the salmon fillets and glaze among 4 dinner plates and serve with the noodles and broccoli as accompaniments.

2. When ready for dessert, cut the spice cake into slices, place a slice on each of 4 dessert plates, and top with some of the sliced peaches. Serve.

Soy- and Honey-Glazed Salmon
Single serving is $1/4$ of total recipe
CALORIES 271; PROTEIN 33g; CARBS 16g;
TOTAL FAT 8g; SAT FAT 1g; CHOLESTEROL 83mg;
SODIUM 807mg; FIBER 0g

hacienda sea bass

avocado and orange salads
warm tortillas
dulce de leche ice cream à la mexicana

menu gameplan

shopping list

Sea bass fillet pieces

Salsa, jarred or refrigerated

Pre-shredded Monterey Jack cheese

Corn chips

Flour tortillas (6-inch diameter)

Prewashed spring or baby greens

Mandarin orange sections

Ripe avocado

Slightly sweet salad dressing, such as French, Catalina, or red wine vinaigrette

Good-quality semisweet chocolate

Dulce de leche ice cream or frozen yogurt

from your pantry

Olive oil

Ground cinnamon

serves 4

step **1** cook the **hacienda sea bass**

step **2** prepare the **warm tortillas**

step **3** assemble the **avocado and orange salads**

step **4** prepare the **dulce de leche ice cream à la mexicana**

step **5** **serve**

luckyforyou Many types of firm-fleshed fish fillets or steaks, such as cod, striped bass, or halibut fillets, can be used in this recipe. Adjust the baking time to suit the thickness. For instance, Chilean sea bass fillets would be delicious but will take 10 minutes longer to bake.

"Target the exact 'heat' level you want in this festive dish by choosing mild or hot salsa and either plain or spicy Monterey Jack cheese."

—minutemeals' Chef Ruth

step 1

cook the **hacienda sea bass**

2 teaspoons olive oil

4 pieces of sea bass fillet (about 5 ounces each)

1 1/3 cups jarred or refrigerated prepared salsa

1 cup (4 ounces) pre-shredded Monterey Jack cheese

1 cup coarsely crushed corn chips

1. Lightly grease a shallow oven-to-table baking dish (just large enough to hold the pieces of fillet in one layer) with the olive oil.

2. Rinse and pat the sea bass pieces dry with paper towels. Place the fish, skin side down, and not quite touching, in a single layer in the prepared dish. Spoon the salsa over the fish, then sprinkle with the cheese.

3. In a plastic bag or in a food processor or blender, coarsely crush enough corn chips to equal 1 cup. Sprinkle the chips over the cheese.

4. Bake in a 425° oven for 15 to 20 minutes, until the fish is opaque and flakes when tested with a fork. The topping should be a rich golden brown.

step 2

prepare the **warm tortillas**

6 to 8 flour tortillas (6-inch diameter)

1. While the fish is baking, wrap the stack of tortillas in foil and heat them alongside the fish without foil.

2. Transfer the tortillas into a napkin-lined basket, cover, and place on the table.

step 3

assemble the **avocado and orange salads**

1 bag (5 ounces) prewashed spring or baby greens

1 can (11 ounces) mandarin orange sections

1 ripe avocado, preferably Hass

2 to 3 tablespoons slightly sweet store-bought salad dressing such as French, Catalina, or red wine vinaigrette

1. Divide the greens among 4 salad plates.

2. Drain the oranges. Halve the avocado, remove the pit, and peel. Cut into thin slices.

3. Arrange slices of avocado on the greens and scatter orange sections over the top. Spoon dressing over each salad. Place the plates on the table.

step 4

prepare the **dulce de leche ice cream à la mexicana**

1 to 2 ounces good-quality semisweet chocolate (or 1 bar)

1 pint dulce de leche ice cream or frozen yogurt

Ground cinnamon for dusting

1. Coarsely grate enough chocolate for sprinkling over 4 servings of ice cream.

2. Remove the ice cream from the freezer to soften slightly before serving.

step 5

serve

1. Transfer the baking dish to the table and serve the sea bass from the dish with the tortillas and salads.

2. When ready for dessert, scoop the ice cream into 4 dessert bowls and sprinkle each with grated chocolate and a dusting of cinnamon. Serve.

Hacienda Sea Bass
Single serving is 1/4 of total recipe
CALORIES 303; PROTEIN 31g; CARBS 9g; TOTAL FAT 16g; SAT FAT 7g; CHOLESTEROL 76mg; SODIUM 649mg; FIBER 2g

cod à la provençale

basmati rice

iceberg, roasted pepper, and olive salad

french bread

orange sorbet with crisp chocolate sandwich cookies

shopping list

Basmati rice

Cod fillets

Diced tomatoes with onion and garlic

Portobello mushroom

Iceberg lettuce

Jarred roasted red peppers

Ripe olives, pitted

Red wine vinaigrette dressing

French bread

Orange sorbet

Crisp chocolate sandwich cookies

from your pantry

Salt and pepper

Olive oil

Dry white wine or fat-free reduced-sodium chicken broth

Herbes de Provence or dried thyme

serves 4

step **1** cook the **basmati rice**

step **2** cook the **cod à la provençale**

step **3** assemble the **iceberg, roasted pepper, and olive salad**

step **4** **serve**

 Mahi mahi, red snapper, or pompano fillets can also be used in this recipe. Adjust the cooking time accordingly.

"Whenever you see the phrase 'à la Provençale' expect bold sunny flavor, tomatoes, and garlic, all of which you get in this flavorful fish dish."

—minutemeals' Chef Ruth

step 1

cook the **basmati rice**

1 cup basmati rice

Salt to taste (optional)

Cook the rice with a pinch of salt, if desired, in a medium saucepan in the amount of water and for the time suggested on the package. Keep warm, covered.

step 2

cook the **cod à la provençale**

4 cod fillets, each 1¼ inches thick and about 6 ounces

1 can (14 ounces) diced tomatoes with onion and garlic

1 large portobello mushroom (6 to 8 ounces)

2 tablespoons olive oil

Salt and pepper to taste

½ cup dry white wine, fat-free reduced-sodium chicken broth, or water

1 teaspoon herbes de Provence or dried thyme

1. Rinse the fillets and pat dry with paper towels. Drain the tomatoes.

2. Stem the portobello mushroom. Rinse the mushroom, pat dry, and thinly slice.

3. Heat 1 tablespoon of the olive oil in a large nonstick skillet over medium heat. Add the mushroom slices and cook until slightly softened, about 2 minutes. Move the mushrooms to the edge of one side of the pan.

4. Add the remaining 1 tablespoon olive oil and the 4 fish fillets to the skillet. Season the fillets with salt and pepper. Cook for 2 minutes on each side. Add the tomatoes, wine or broth or water, and herbes de Provence or thyme and bring to a boil. Reduce the heat to medium, cover, and simmer until the fish is opaque in the thickest part and flakes when tested with a fork, 6 to 8 minutes.

step 3

assemble the **iceberg, roasted pepper, and olive salad**

1 small head iceberg lettuce

1 jar (about 7 ounces) roasted red peppers

¼ cup small pitted ripe olives

2 to 3 tablespoons store-bought red wine vinaigrette dressing

Salt and pepper to taste

1. Core the iceberg lettuce and tear it into bite-sized pieces. Place in salad bowl.

2. Drain the red peppers and cut into strips. Drain the ripe olives. Add the pepper strips and olives to the salad bowl. Drizzle with the vinaigrette, season with salt and pepper, and toss. Place the salad bowl on the table.

step 4

serve

1. Divide the cod and sauce evenly among 4 dinner plates. Serve.

2. Fluff the rice with a fork, transfer it to a serving bowl, and place on the table . Serve the French bread on a bread board.

3. When ready for dessert, scoop the sorbet into 4 dessert bowls and garnish each with 1 or 2 chocolate cookies. Serve.

Cod à la Provençale
Single serving is ¼ of total recipe
CALORIES 186; PROTEIN 20g; CARBS 6g; TOTAL FAT 8g; SAT FAT 1g; CHOLESTEROL 45mg; SODIUM 426mg; FIBER 1g

grilled swordfish
with mango, melon, and grape salsa

sliced tomato and radish salad

semolina bread

chocolate swirl ice cream

menu
gameplan

shopping list

Ripe mango

Scallions

Jalapeño pepper

Limes (for juice)

Swordfish steaks

Ripe beefsteak tomatoes

Red or white radishes

Semolina or other crusty bread

Chocolate swirl ice cream

from the salad bar

Cantaloupe or honeydew melon chunks (or from the produce department)

Seedless green grapes (or from the produce department)

from your pantry

Olive oil

Salt and pepper

Vinaigrette dressing, store-bought or homemade

serves 4

beforeyoustart
Preheat the broiler.

step **1** make the **mango, melon, and grape salsa**

step **2** cook the **grilled swordfish**

step **3** assemble the **sliced tomato and radish salad**

step **4** serve

luckyforyou When fresh melon is no longer in season, use precut fresh pineapple in the salsa.

"A velvety, juicy fruit salsa works in perfect contrast with fish steaks or fillets. Another time, substitute fresh tuna or shark steaks for the swordfish."

—minutemeals' Chef Ruth

step 1

make the **mango, melon, and grape salsa**

1/2 of 1 ripe mango
(about 1/2 pound)

1 small bunch seedless
green grapes

4 scallions

1 jalapeño pepper

1 cup (4 ounces) cantaloupe or
honeydew melon chunks

1/4 cup fresh lime juice
(1 large or 2 small limes)

4 teaspoons olive oil

Salt and pepper to taste

1. Peel, seed, and cube the mango half.

2. Cut enough green grapes in half to equal 1 cup.

3. Trim the scallions and thinly slice, using most of the tender green parts. Seed and very finely mince the jalapeño pepper.

4. Place the melon, mango, grapes, scallions, and jalapeño pepper in a medium bowl.

5. Squeeze enough lime juice to measure 1/4 cup. Pour 3 tablespoons of the juice into the fruit mixture and stir to combine. (Reserve the remaining 1 tablespoon lime juice for the swordfish.) Add the olive oil to the salsa mixture, season with salt and pepper, and mix well. Chill.

step 2

cook the **grilled swordfish**

4 swordfish steaks (each about
3/4 inch thick and 5 to 6 ounces)

1 tablespoon fresh lime juice
(reserved from salsa recipe)

2 teaspoons olive oil

Salt and pepper to taste

1. Preheat the broiler. Line the broiler pan with aluminum foil.

2. Rinse the swordfish steaks and pat dry.

3. Brush both sides of the swordfish steaks with the remaining 1 tablespoon lime juice and olive oil. Place the swordfish on the broiler-pan rack and season with salt and pepper. Broil about 5 inches from the heat until just cooked through, about 6 to 8 minutes, turning once during cooking.

step 3

assemble the **sliced tomato and radish salad**

2 large ripe beefsteak tomatoes

1 small bunch red or white
radishes

2 tablespoons vinaigrette
dressing

Salt and pepper to taste

1. Rinse the tomatoes and pat dry. Cut the tomatoes into thick slices and divide the slices among 4 salad plates.

2. Clean, trim, and slice the bunch of radishes. Scatter the radish slices over the tomatoes. Drizzle each salad with vinaigrette and season with salt and pepper. Place the salads on the table.

step 4

serve

1. Place a piece of swordfish on each of 4 dinner plates and spoon some of the chilled salsa around it, dividing the salsa evenly. Serve at once.

2. Serve the bread on a bread board, warmed ahead of time, if desired.

3. When ready for dessert, scoop the ice cream into 4 dessert bowls and serve.

Grilled Swordfish with Mango, Melon, and Grape Salsa
Single serving is 1/4 of total recipe
CALORIES 266; PROTEIN 20g; CARBS 23g;
TOTAL FAT 11g; SAT FAT 2g; CHOLESTEROL 38mg;
SODIUM 386mg; FIBER 2g

shrimp and feta casseroles

cucumber and kalamata olive salad

warm pita bread

baklava

shopping list

Shallots

Diced tomatoes

Medium shrimp, peeled and deveined

Crumbled feta cheese

Light cream or half-and-half

Pita breads

Prewashed mixed spring or baby greens

Kalamata olives, pitted

Baklava (from the bakery)

from the salad bar

Cucumber slices

Red onion slices

from your pantry

Nonstick vegetable cooking spray

Olive oil

Dried oregano

Eggs

Hot pepper sauce

Salt and pepper

Grated Parmesan cheese

Red wine vinegar

serves 4

beforeyoustart

Preheat the oven to 400°F to bake the casseroles.

step 1 make the **shrimp and feta casseroles**

step 2 prepare the **warm pita bread**

step 3 assemble the **cucumber and kalamata salad**

step 4 **serve**

luckyforyou

If you don't have 4 small gratin dishes, bake the shrimp and feta mixture in a shallow 2-quart casserole and allow about 18 minutes for the larger dish to bake.

"Devotees of Greek cooking will recognize the inspiration for these casseroles: Garides me Saltsa. Fresh oregano, if available, will add authentic flavor to the dish."

—minutemeals' Chef Ruth

step 1

make the **shrimp and feta casseroles**

Nonstick vegetable cooking spray

3 tablespoons chopped shallots

1 can (14 ounces) drained diced tomatoes

1 tablespoon olive oil

1/2 teaspoon crumbled dried oregano

1 pound peeled and deveined medium shrimp

A heaping 1/3 cup finely crumbled feta cheese (4 ounces)

3 large eggs

2/3 cup light cream or half-and-half

1/4 teaspoon hot pepper sauce

Salt and pepper to taste

4 tablespoons grated Parmesan cheese

1. Preheat the oven to 400°F. Lightly spray 4 shallow 1 1/2- to 2-cup gratin dishes or individual casseroles with nonstick vegetable cooking spray.

2. Chop enough shallots to measure 3 tablespoons. Drain the tomatoes, reserving the juice for another use such as an addition to soup.

3. Heat the olive oil in a medium nonstick skillet over medium-high heat. Add the shallots and cook,

stirring frequently, for 1 minute, until nearly softened. Stir in the tomatoes and oregano and heat through, about 1 minute.

4. Meanwhile, divide the shrimp among the 4 prepared baking dishes, spreading them in a single layer. Spoon the hot tomato mixture over them. Sprinkle with the feta, dividing it equally.

5. In a medium bowl, whisk the eggs together with the cream and hot pepper sauce. Season with salt and pepper. Pour the egg mixture evenly over the shrimp and tomatoes, dividing it equally among the casseroles. Sprinkle each with 1 tablespoon grated Parmesan.

6. Bake for about 12 minutes, or until the custard is set around the edges but is still saucy in the center. Remove from the oven and let stand a few minutes before serving.

step 2

warm the **pita bread**

4 to 6 pita breads

Wrap the pita breads loosely in foil and place in the oven to warm with the casseroles for the last 5 minutes of baking. Cut the pitas into wedges and arrange in a napkin-lined basket. Cover and place the basket on the table.

step 3

assemble the **cucumber and kalamata salad**

1 bag (5 ounces) prewashed mixed spring or baby greens

1 cup cucumber slices

1/4 cup red onion slices

1/2 cup pitted kalamata olives

2 tablespoons olive oil

1 tablespoon red wine vinegar

Salt and pepper to taste

Place the salad greens in a shallow salad bowl. Top with the cucumber and onion slices, and scatter the olives over all. Drizzle with the olive oil and vinegar and season with salt and pepper. Place the bowl on the table, with 4 salad plates.

step 4

serve

1. Place a gratin dish on each of 4 dinner plates and serve.

2. Toss the salad at the table.

3. When ready for dessert, place a piece of the baklava on each of 4 dessert plates and serve.

Shrimp and Feta Casseroles
Single serving is 1/4 of total recipe
CALORIES 330; PROTEIN 28g; CARBS 8g;
TOTAL FAT 20g; SAT FAT 10g; CHOLESTEROL 363mg;
SODIUM 754mg; FIBER 1g

☆ caribbean shrimp

basmati rice
stir-fried spinach
mango sorbet with coconut macaroons

menu
gameplan

shopping list

Basmati rice

Large or jumbo shrimp, peeled and deveined

Scallions

Fresh mint or parsley

Limes

Pineapple chunks, fresh (from the salad bar or produce department) or canned juice-packed

Prewashed baby spinach

Mango sorbet

Coconut macaroons

from your pantry

Turmeric (optional)

Garlic

Butter

Dark rum

Salt and pepper

Hot pepper sauce

Olive oil

serves 4

step	1	cook the **basmati rice**
step	2	cook the **caribbean shrimp**
step	3	cook the **stir-fried spinach**
step	4	**serve**

headsup
Watch out for peeled and deveined shrimp that have been dipped in chemicals, often done to prevent moisture from seeping out of the shrimp. The chemicals are safe, but can give a too-slick feel and an odd taste to the shrimp. Ask your fish seller to show you the box, and look for "additive free."

"The national appetite for shrimp seems to be ever-increasing, with quality imports arriving from far afield."

—minutemeals' Chef Ruth

step 1
cook the **basmati rice**

1 cup basmati rice

1/8 teaspoon turmeric (optional)

Cook the basmati rice in a medium saucepan in the amount of water and for the time suggested on the package, adding the turmeric to the water, if desired.

step 2
cook the **caribbean shrimp**

1 1/2 pounds peeled and deveined large or jumbo shrimp

3 scallions

3 garlic cloves

1/3 cup finely chopped fresh mint or parsley

4 or 5 large limes (enough for 1/4 cup juice plus slices for garnish)

4 tablespoons butter

1/2 cup dark rum or 1/4 cup each rum and pineapple juice or 1/2 cup pineapple juice

1/4 teaspoon hot pepper sauce

Salt and pepper

1 cup precut fresh or drained canned juice-packed pineapple chunks

1. Rinse the shrimp and pat dry with paper towels. Chop the scallions. Mince the garlic. Chop enough fresh mint to measure 1/3 cup. Squeeze enough juice from the limes to measure 1/4 cup; cut 1 lime into slices for garnish.

2. Melt the butter in a large non-stick skillet over medium heat. Add the shrimp, scallions, and garlic. Cook, stirring often, for about 2 minutes, or until the scallions are wilted and the shrimp are beginning to turn pink.

3. Stir in the mint, dark rum, lime juice, and hot pepper sauce. Season with salt and pepper. Bring to a boil and cook until the shrimp are just tender and opaque in the thickest part, about 1 minute more.

4. With a slotted spoon, transfer the shrimp to a bowl. Let the sauce boil 1 or 2 minutes or until slightly reduced. Return the shrimp to the skillet and remove the pan from the heat. Add the pineapple chunks and stir to combine and heat through.

step 3
cook the **stir-fried spinach**

1 tablespoon olive oil

2 bags (10 ounces each) prewashed baby spinach

Salt and pepper to taste

Heat the olive oil in a large skillet or wok over high heat until hot but not smoking. Add the spinach and stir-fry it for 2 to 3 minutes, or until hot and just wilted. Season with salt and pepper. Transfer to a serving dish and place on the table.

step 4
serve

1. Divide the basmati rice among 4 dinner plates and top with the shrimp, pineapple, and sauce, dividing them equally with spinach as an accompaniment. Garnish each plate with lime slices and serve.

2. When ready for dessert, scoop the mango sorbet into 4 small bowls and serve with the macaroons.

Caribbean Shrimp
Single serving is 1/4 of total recipe
CALORIES 274; PROTEIN 27g; CARBS 8g; TOTAL FAT 13g; SAT FAT 8g; CHOLESTEROL 273mg; SODIUM 292mg; FIBER 1g

shrimp, snow pea, and straw mushroom stir-fry

angel hair pasta

orange-scented grapefruit sections and pecan butter cookies

menu gameplan

shopping list

Angel hair pasta

Jarred grapefruit sections (in the refrigerated section of the produce department)

Orange-flavored liqueur or orange or vanilla extract

Pecan butter cookies

Canned straw mushrooms

Large shrimp, peeled and deveined

from the salad bar

Snow peas

Red pepper slices

from your pantry

Salt

Toasted sesame oil

Fat-free reduced-sodium chicken broth

Lite soy sauce

Cornstarch

Garlic

Vegetable oil

serves 4

step	1	cook the **angel hair pasta**
step	2	plate the **grapefruit sections and cookies**
step	3	make the **shrimp, snow pea, and straw mushroom stir-fry**
step	4	**serve**

headsup

The trick with stir-fry dishes is to have all the ingredients prepared, measured, and set up near the range before starting. Then each ingredient can go into the skillet or wok at just the right time to retain its desired crisp or tender texture and bright color. Make the guests wait for the stir-fry, not the reverse!

"This menu is wonderful for company, because the cook will also be able to enjoy the party. That's how easy these dishes are to make."

—minutemeals' Chef Ruth

step 1

cook the **angel hair pasta**

4 quarts water

Salt to taste

8 ounces angel hair pasta

$1/2$ teaspoon toasted sesame oil

Pour the water into a large pot, salt lightly, and cover. Bring to a boil over high heat. Add the pasta, stir to separate the strands, and cook according to the directions on the package, until *al dente*. Drain, transfer to a serving bowl, and add the sesame oil. Toss until coated. Place the bowl on the table.

step 2

plate the **grapefruit sections and cookies**

1 jar (24 ounces) red grapefruit sections in slightly sweetened juice

4 tablespoons orange-flavored liqueur or orange or vanilla extract

Pecan butter cookies

1. Spoon the grapefruit sections into 4 dessert bowls. Drizzle each with 1 tablespoon of the orange-flavored liqueur or a few drops of orange or vanilla extract. Chill until serving time.

2. Arrange the pecan cookies on a small serving platter.

step 3

make the **shrimp, snow pea, and straw mushroom stir-fry**

$2/3$ cup fat-free reduced-sodium chicken broth

2 tablespoons lite soy sauce

4 teaspoons cornstarch

6 ounces fresh snow peas

3 garlic cloves

1 can (16 ounces) straw mushrooms

1 pound peeled and deveined large shrimp

2 tablespoons vegetable oil

2 teaspoons toasted sesame oil

1 cup thin red pepper slices

1. In a small bowl, stir together the chicken broth, soy sauce, and cornstarch.

2. Trim the stem ends from the snow peas. Thinly slice the garlic. Drain the straw mushrooms. Rinse the shrimp and pat dry with paper towels.

3. Heat the vegetable and sesame oils in a large heavy skillet or wok over high heat. Add the pepper slices and garlic. Stir-fry for 3 minutes, until the pepper slices are slightly wilted but are still crisp-tender. Add the snow peas, straw mushrooms, shrimp and stir-fry until the shrimp turn pink, 2 to 4 minutes.

4. Stir the broth mixture to recombine, and stir it into the skillet. Cook, stirring constantly, until the sauce is thickened and bubbly, about 1 minute. Remove the pan from the heat.

step 4

serve

1. Divide the pasta among 4 pasta bowls or dinner plates. Spoon the shrimp stir-fry over each serving of pasta and serve at once.

2. When ready for dessert, serve the chilled bowls of grapefruit sections with the pecan butter cookies as an accompaniment.

Shrimp, Snow Pea, and Straw Mushroom Stir-Fry
Single serving is $1/4$ of total recipe
CALORIES 236; PROTEIN 23g; CARBS 13g; TOTAL FAT 11g; SAT FAT 1g; CHOLESTEROL 161mg; SODIUM 925mg; FIBER 4g

tuna patties
saucy zucchini salsa
vegetable chips
carrot cake

menu
gameplan

serves 4

step **1** make the **tuna patties**

step **2** cook the **saucy zucchini salsa**

step **3** **serve**

shopping list

Chives or green part of scallion

Chunk light water-packed tuna

Zucchini

Salsa

Tomato sauce

Vegetable chips

Carrot cake (from the bakery)

from your pantry

Dried seasoned bread crumbs

Mayonnaise

Egg

Pickle relish

Cayenne pepper

Light olive or vegetable oil

Dried thyme

Sugar

luckyforyou Many supermarkets now have extensive bakeries. If you can't find carrot cake, substitute morning glory muffins. You can frost them with a quick mixture of soft cream cheese and confectioners' sugar, or just dust them with the sugar, if you're running out of time.

"Every cook needs a menu like this to keep on hand for emergencies. Since it uses mostly pantry items, you can create it without having to shop."

—minutemeals' Chef Paul

step 1

make the **tuna patties**

1/2 cup dried seasoned bread crumbs

2 tablespoons snipped chives or green part of scallion

1/4 cup mayonnaise

1 egg yolk

1 tablespoon pickle relish

1/8 teaspoon cayenne pepper

2 cans (6 ounces each) drained chunk light water-packed tuna

2 tablespoons light olive or vegetable oil

1. Spread 1/4 cup of the bread crumbs in an even layer on a sheet of waxed paper; reserve. With kitchen scissors, snip enough chives or green part of scallion to measure 2 tablespoons.

2. In a medium bowl, stir together the mayonnaise, egg yolk, chives or scallion pieces, pickle relish, and cayenne pepper until combined.

3. Drain the tuna, pressing down on the lids to remove excess liquid. Flake the tuna into the mayonnaise mixture in the bowl. Add the remaining 1/4 cup bread crumbs and stir until well combined.

4. Drop 1/4 of the tuna mixture onto the crumbs on the waxed paper and form into an oval patty (about 5 × 3 inches). Coat both sides in crumbs. Repeat with the remaining tuna mixture and crumbs.

5. Heat the olive or vegetable oil in a large nonstick skillet over medium heat. Add the patties and cook until golden brown and heated through, about 3 minutes per side. Remove the pan from the heat.

step 2

cook the **saucy zucchini salsa**

1 pound zucchini

1 tablespoon olive oil

1/2 teaspoon dried thyme

1/2 cup prepared salsa

1/2 cup canned tomato sauce

1/2 teaspoon sugar

1. Trim the zucchini, quarter each lengthwise, and thinly slice.

2. Place the olive oil in a nonstick skillet over medium heat. Add the zucchini and thyme and cook for 5 to 6 minutes, stirring occasionally, until almost tender.

3. Stir in the salsa, tomato sauce, and sugar. Cook for 2 minutes, or until the zucchini is just tender and the sauce is heated through. Transfer to a serving bowl and place on the table.

step 3

serve

1. Place a tuna patty on each of 4 dinner plates and add a handful of vegetable chips as an accompaniment. Serve, with the warm zucchini salsa.

2. When ready for dessert, cut the carrot cake into generous slices and serve on 4 dessert plates.

Tuna Patties
Single serving is 1/4 of total recipe
CALORIES 316; PROTEIN 21g; CARBS 12g; TOTAL FAT 20g; SAT FAT 3g; CHOLESTEROL 83mg; SODIUM 749mg; FIBER 1g

tuna noodle skillet casserole

basil peas with roasted peppers

fresh pears and soft molasses cookies

menu
gameplan

shopping list

Wide egg noodles

Celery

Dried common mushrooms

Chives or scallions

Water-packed tuna

Reduced-fat sour cream

Potato chips

Frozen peas

Jarred roasted pepper strips

Fresh basil

Ripe pears (4)

Soft molasses cookies

from your pantry

Vegetable broth

Dried thyme

Salt and pepper

Butter

serves 4

beforeyoustart

Bring a large pot of water, covered, to a boil over high heat to cook the noodles.

step **1** cook the **tuna noodle skillet casserole**

step **2** prepare the **basil peas with roasted peppers**

step **3** **serve**

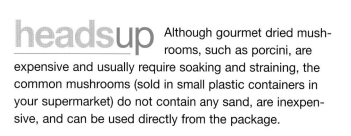

headsup Although gourmet dried mushrooms, such as porcini, are expensive and usually require soaking and straining, the common mushrooms (sold in small plastic containers in your supermarket) do not contain any sand, are inexpensive, and can be used directly from the package.

"This is a great base recipe for any creamy pasta dish. You can substitute cooked chicken or ham for the tuna."

—minutemeals' Chef Paul

step 1

cook the **tuna noodle skillet casserole**

3 quarts water

12 ounces wide egg noodles

3 stalks celery

1 container (1/2 ounce) dried common mushrooms

1 cup vegetable broth

1 teaspoon dried thyme

1 bunch chives or 3 scallions

1 can (12 ounces) water-packed tuna

1 1/2 cups reduced-fat sour cream

Salt and pepper to taste

1/3 cup crushed potato chips

1. Pour the water into a large pot, cover, and bring to a boil over high heat. Add the egg noodles, stir, and cook according to the directions on the package. Reserve about 1 cup of the cooking water and drain the noodles well.

2. Meanwhile, thinly slice the celery and place in a large skillet. Crumble the dried mushrooms into the skillet. Add the vegetable broth and thyme, cover, and bring to a boil over medium-high heat. Uncover and simmer for 6 minutes.

3. Snip the chives or slice the scallions. Stir the chives or scallions and undrained tuna into the skillet until well combined. Remove the pan from the heat.

4. Put the sour cream in a medium bowl and stir in a little of the hot liquid from the skillet. Stir until blended.

5. Stir the sour cream mixture into the skillet until blended. Add the pasta, and season to taste with salt and pepper. If the noodles seem dry, stir in some of the reserved cooking water, a tablespoon at a time, until moistened. Scatter the crushed potato chips on top.

step 2

prepare the **basil peas with roasted peppers**

1 bag (16 ounces) frozen peas

1 jar (7 ounces) roasted pepper strips

2 tablespoons softened butter

Salt and pepper to taste

1/4 cup fresh basil leaves

1. Place the peas in a 1-quart microwave-safe dish and add 3 tablespoons water. Cover with vented plastic or lid and microwave on High for 8 minutes. Place the jarred pepper strips in a large colander. Add the peas and drain well.

2. Transfer the vegetables to a serving bowl. Add the butter and season with salt and pepper.

3. Rinse the basil leaves and pat dry.

step 3

serve

1. Place the skillet of tuna noodle casserole on the table and serve from the skillet.

2. Thinly slice the basil leaves, add to the peas, and stir until combined. Serve as a side dish.

3. When ready for dessert, place the pears and cookies on a platter and serve with 4 dessert plates and knives.

Tuna Noodle Skillet Casserole
Single serving is 1/4 of total recipe

CALORIES 571; PROTEIN 38g; CARBS 65g; TOTAL FAT 17g; SAT FAT 8g; CHOLESTEROL 141mg; SODIUM 1147mg; FIBER 5g

tonnato alfredo
with sun-dried tomatoes
artichoke and olive salad
amaretti cookies

shopping list

Elbow macaroni or medium shells

Frozen peas

Light chunk water-packed tuna

Refrigerated Alfredo sauce

Sun-dried tomatoes, slivered

Cherry tomatoes (from the salad bar)

Kalamata olives, pitted

Jarred marinated artichoke hearts

Prewashed Italian-style blend salad greens

Amaretti cookies

from your pantry

Salt and pepper

Grated Parmesan cheese

Balsamic vinegar

serves 4

beforeyoustart

Bring a large pot of water, covered, to a boil over high heat to cook the pasta.

step	1	cook the **tonnato alfredo with sun-dried tomatoes**
step	2	assemble the **artichoke and olive salad**
step	3	**serve**

luckyforyou A mini-processor, called for to combine the sauce, makes for quicker clean-up. If you don't have one, use a blender (standard or hand-held) or a regular food processor.

"This pasta dish is great served either hot or cold. To serve it cold, rinse the pasta and peas with cold water and drain well. Proceed as directed."

—minutemeals' Chef Paul

step 1

cook the **tonnato alfredo with sun-dried tomatoes**

3 quarts water

Salt to taste

12 ounces elbow macaroni or medium shells

1 package (10 ounces) frozen peas

1 can (6 ounces) light chunk water-packed tuna

1 container (10 ounces) refrigerated Alfredo sauce

1/3 cup slivered sun-dried tomatoes

1/4 cup grated Parmesan, plus additional for serving

1. Pour the water into a large pot, salt lightly, and cover. Bring to a boil over high heat. Add the pasta, stir to separate, and cook according to the directions on the package for 8 minutes. Add the peas during the last 1 minute of cooking. Reserve about 1 cup of the cooking liquid and drain the pasta and peas well in a colander.

2. Meanwhile, drain the tuna and place in a mini or regular-sized food processor. Add the Alfredo sauce and blend until smooth. Spoon the sauce into a pasta serving bowl. Stir in the sun-dried tomatoes and grated Parmesan.

3. Add the hot pasta and peas to the tuna Alfredo sauce and toss well to combine. If desired, stir in some of the reserved cooking liquid, 1 tablespoon at a time, for a saucy consistency. Cover loosely to keep warm.

step 2

assemble the **artichoke and olive salad**

1 cup cherry tomatoes

1/4 cup pitted kalamata olives

1 jar (6 ounces) marinated artichoke hearts

2 tablespoons balsamic vinegar

1 package (5 ounces) prewashed Italian-style blend salad greens

Salt and pepper to taste

1. Rinse the tomatoes and pat dry. Halve the tomatoes and olives. Place both in a medium salad bowl. Add the artichokes and their liquid and the vinegar, tossing until combined. Add salt and pepper to taste.

2. Place the salad greens in the bowl; do not toss until right before serving.

step 3

serve

1. Place the bowl of Tonnato Alfredo on the table with 4 large pasta bowls or plates. Serve with additional grated Parmesan for topping, if desired.

2. Toss the salad and place the bowl on the table with 4 salad plates.

3. When ready for dessert, arrange the amaretti on a plate. Serve.

Tonnato Alfredo with Sun-Dried Tomatoes
Single serving is 1/4 of total recipe

CALORIES 711; PROTEIN 32g; CARBS 77g; TOTAL FAT 31g; SAT FAT 13g; CHOLESTEROL 67mg; SODIUM 1264mg; FIBER 7g

minute
3 ways

pasta, bean, and vegetable menus

meals
to dinner

pasta
with white beans and sun-dried tomato pesto

broccoli rabe

peanut butter ice cream sundaes

shopping list

Macaroni

Small white beans

Fresh parsley

Prepared sun-dried tomato pesto

Broccoli rabe

Peanut butter ice cream

Salted peanuts, chopped

Chocolate sprinkles

Peanut butter cookies

from your pantry

Salt and pepper

Fruity olive oil

Grated Parmesan cheese

 luckyforyou Sun-dried tomato pesto can be found in the super-market in jars in the specialty Italian foods section. Use as a sauce, a spread, or as a flavor enhancer in salad dressings or soups.

menu gameplan

serves 4

beforeyoustart

Bring a large pot of water, covered, to a boil over high heat to cook the pasta.

step **1** cook the **pasta**

step **2** cook the **broccoli rabe**

step **3** prepare the **peanut butter ice cream sundaes**

step **4** **serve**

"Pesto, whether it's made with fresh basil or sun-dried tomatoes, is synonymous with big flavor. It makes this easy vegetarian pasta sauce."

—minutemeals' Chef Hillary

step 1

cook the **pasta with white beans and sun-dried tomato pesto**

3 quarts water

Salt to taste

12 ounces macaroni

2 cans (15^1/2 ounces each) small white beans

^{1}/2 cup chopped fresh parsley

3 tablespoons fruity olive oil

^{1}/4 cup prepared sun-dried tomato pesto

Salt and pepper to taste

^{1}/4 cup grated Parmesan cheese

1. Pour the water into a large pot, salt lightly, and cover. Bring to a boil over high heat. Add the macaroni, stir, and cook according to the directions on the package for 6 to 8 minutes, or until *al dente*. Remove ^{1}/2 cup of the pasta cooking water and reserve. Drain in a colander.

2. Rinse and drain the white beans. Chop enough parsley to measure ^{1}/2 cup.

3. In the pasta cooking pot, warm the olive oil over medium heat. Stir in the beans, pesto, and parsley, and season with salt and pepper. Heat through, stirring often. Add the macaroni and enough of the pasta cooking water to prevent the pasta from sticking. Sprinkle with the Parmesan, and remove the pan from the heat.

step 2

cook the **broccoli rabe**

1 bunch (about 1^1/2 pounds) broccoli rabe

1 tablespoon fruity olive oil

Salt and pepper to taste

1. Remove and discard the tough stems from the broccoli rabe and cut it into 2-inch pieces.

2. Fill a large skillet with ^{1}/2 inch water and salt lightly. Bring the water to a boil over high heat, covered. Add the broccoli and cook, stirring often, until tender, for 4 to 6 minutes. Drain and transfer to a serving bowl. Drizzle with the olive oil and season with salt and pepper. Place the bowl on the table, with 4 small plates.

step 3

prepare the **peanut butter ice cream sundaes**

1 pint peanut butter ice cream

^{1}/3 cup chopped salted peanuts

^{1}/4 cup chocolate sprinkles

4 oversized peanut butter cookies

1. Remove the ice cream from freezer to soften.

2. Scoop ice cream onto each of 4 dessert bowls. Sprinkle each with peanuts and chocolate sprinkles. Place the bowls in the freezer until serving time.

step 4

serve

1. Serve the pasta in pasta bowls, with the broccoli rabe as an accompaniment.

2. When ready for dessert, garnish each ice cream sundae with a peanut butter cookie. Serve.

Pasta with White Beans and Sun-Dried Tomato Pesto
Single serving is ^{1}/4 of total recipe

CALORIES 651; PROTEIN 25g; CARBS 101g; TOTAL FAT 16g; SAT FAT 3g; CHOLESTEROL 5mg; SODIUM 607mg; FIBER 12g

vegetable "lo mein"

vegetable egg rolls with spicy mustard

almond pound cake delight

menu gameplan

serves 4

step	1	prepare the **vegetable egg rolls with spicy mustard**
step	2	make the **vegetable "lo mein"**
step	3	prepare the **almond pound cake delight**
step	4	**serve**

shopping list

Frozen vegetable egg rolls
(1 per person)

Firm tofu

Gingerroot

Fresh spaghetti

Frozen Oriental-style
vegetables

Scallions

Pound cake

Prepared vanilla pudding

Chinese-style almond
cookies

from your pantry

Dried mustard

Honey

Toasted sesame oil

Vegetable oil

Vegetable broth or fat-free
reduced-sodium chicken
broth

Teriyaki sauce

Dried red pepper flakes

Amaretto liqueur

luckyforyou Fresh pasta keeps the
cooking time here to the
absolute minimum. Try a flavored pasta for a change.

"This brothy variation on lo mein has less oil than the traditional preparation. It's definitely 'slurpy'! Add shrimp for a nonvegetarian twist."

—minutemeals' Chef Hillary

step 1

prepare the **vegetable egg rolls with spicy mustard**

2 packages (6 ounces each) frozen vegetable egg rolls

1 tablespoon dried mustard

3 tablespoons water

1 teaspoon honey

1. Heat the egg rolls according to the directions on the package.

2. In a small bowl, stir the mustard and water together until smooth. Stir in the honey.

step 2

make the **vegetable "lo mein"**

8 ounces firm tofu

1-inch piece gingerroot

1 tablespoon toasted sesame oil

1 tablespoon vegetable oil

4 cups vegetable broth or fat-free low-sodium chicken broth

3 tablespoons teriyaki sauce

1/4 teaspoon dried red pepper flakes

1 package (9 ounces) fresh spaghetti

1 bag (16 ounces) frozen Oriental-style vegetables

2 scallions for garnish

1. Cut the tofu into 1-inch cubes. Peel and grate the ginger.

2. In a large heavy skillet, heat the sesame and vegetable oils over medium-high heat. Add the tofu and cook, turning often, until lightly browned, about 3 minutes. Remove from the heat.

3. In a large saucepan, combine the ginger, broth, teriyaki sauce, and pepper flakes. Cover and bring to a boil over high heat.

4. Add the spaghetti, stir to separate the strands, and cook, stirring often, for 3 minutes. Stir in the browned tofu and frozen vegetables. Cover and bring to a boil. Reduce the heat and simmer for 2 minutes, until the noodles are tender and the vegetables are heated through. Remove the pan from the heat.

5. Thinly slice the scallions.

step 3

prepare the **almond pound cake delight**

4 slices of pound cake

1/4 cup Amaretto liqueur or orange juice

8 ounces prepared vanilla pudding

4 Chinese-style almond cookies

Place a slice of pound cake on each of 4 dessert plates. Sprinkle each with 1 tablespoon Amaretto or orange juice.

step 4

serve

1. Ladle the "lo mein" into 4 pasta bowls and garnish each with sliced scallion. Serve.

2. Place 1 egg roll on each of 4 small plates and serve at once with the spicy mustard for dipping.

3. When ready for dessert, top each slice of pound cake with vanilla pudding, and crush an almond cookie over the top. Serve.

Vegetable "Lo Mein"
Single serving is 1/4 of total recipe
CALORIES 372; PROTEIN 18g; CARBS 51g;
TOTAL FAT 12g; SAT FAT 1g; CHOLESTEROL 47mg;
SODIUM 1574mg; FIBER 5g

chili spaghetti
mixed green salad
peach pie à la mode

shopping list

Thin spaghetti

Lean ground beef

Hormel® vegetarian chili

Pre-shredded Cheddar cheese

Ripe tomatoes

Prewashed salad greens

Peach pie

Vanilla ice cream

from the salad bar

Mushroom slices

Red onion slices

from your pantry

Salt and pepper

Olive oil

Chili powder

Ground cumin

Red wine vinegar

Vinaigrette dressing, store-bought

serves 6

beforeyoustart

Preheat the oven to 300°F to heat the pie.

step 1   cook the **chili spaghetti**

step 2   assemble the **mixed green salad**

step 3   heat the **peach pie**

step 4   **serve**

 luckyforyou Canned chili here instantly perks up the flavor of this dish (so you don't have to bother yourself with a long list of ingredients). There are many different brands of chili on the market, ranging from vegetarian to meat and from mild to spicy. Experiment.

"This chili literally takes minutes to prepare. If you're in a rush, skip the spaghetti and serve the chili in a large corn tortilla shell."

—minutemeals' Chef Hillary

step 1

cook the **chili spaghetti**

4 quarts water

Salt

1 pound thin spaghetti

2 teaspoons olive oil

1 pound 85% lean ground beef

2 teaspoons chili powder

1 teaspoon ground cumin

1 can (15 ounces) Hormel® vegetarian chili

1/2 cup water

2 tablespoons red wine vinegar

Salt and pepper to taste

1 cup pre-shredded Cheddar cheese

1. Pour the water into a large pot, salt lightly, and cover. Bring to a boil over high heat. Add the spaghetti, stir to separate, and cook 6 to 8 minutes until just *al dente*. Drain in a colander and return to the cooking pot.

2. In a large deep heavy skillet, heat the olive oil over high heat. Add the beef and cook for 3 to 5 minutes, breaking it up with a fork and stirring, until nicely browned. Stir in the chili powder and cumin

and cook for 1 minute. Stir in the canned chili, water, and vinegar. Bring to a boil and simmer 1 to 2 minutes, or until slightly thickened. Season with salt and pepper.

3. Add the chili to the cooked pasta and toss well to combine. Sprinkle the pasta with the grated Cheddar.

step 2

assemble the **mixed green salad**

2 ripe medium tomatoes

6 cups prewashed salad greens

1/2 cup mushroom slices

1/2 cup red onion slices

2 to 4 tablespoons store-bought vinaigrette dressing

Salt and pepper to taste

1. Rinse the tomatoes and pat dry. Cut the tomatoes into wedges.

2. In a salad bowl, combine the salad greens, mushroom and onion slices, tomato wedges, and dressing. Season with salt and pepper and toss to coat. Place the bowl on the table, with 4 salad plates.

step 3

heat the **peach pie**

1 peach pie

1 pint vanilla ice cream

1. Preheat the oven to 300°F. Place the pie in the oven to heat while having dinner.

2. Remove the ice cream from the freezer to soften slightly.

step 4

serve

1. Serve the chili spaghetti in 4 pasta bowls, with the salad as an accompaniment.

2. When ready for dessert, cut the peach pie into 6 slices, place each on a dessert plate, and top with a scoop of the vanilla ice cream. Serve.

Chili Spaghetti
Single serving is 1/6 of total recipe
CALORIES 583; PROTEIN 33g. CARBS 72g;
TOTAL FAT 18g; Sat FAT 8g; CHOLESTEROL 70mg;
SODIUM 601mg; FIBER 7g

ravioli
with shrimp, peas, and tomato cream
antipasto salad
raspberry gelato

menu
gameplan

shopping list

Refrigerated or frozen
large cheese ravioli

Frozen petite peas

Fresh basil

Thick-and-chunky-style
pasta sauce

Heavy cream

Medium or small shrimp,
peeled and deveined

Jarred marinated artichoke
hearts

Jarred roasted red peppers

Marinated olives

Celery slices
(from the salad bar)

Prewashed colorful mixed
salad greens

Raspberry gelato

from your pantry

Salt and pepper

Dried red pepper flakes
(optional)

Balsamic vinegar

serves 4

beforeyoustart

Bring a large pot of water, covered, to a
boil over high heat to cook the ravioli.

step **1** make the **ravioli with shrimp, peas, and tomato cream**

step **2** assemble the **antipasto salad**

step **3** **serve**

headsup
Cook the shrimp in the tomato
cream sauce until they are
pink and just cooked through. Shrimp overcook easily and
will continue to cook as they sit.

step 1

make the **ravioli with shrimp, peas, and tomato cream**

4 quarts water

Salt to taste

1 package (1 pound 4 ounces) refrigerated large cheese ravioli or about 1 pound frozen cheese ravioli

1 package (10 ounces) frozen petite peas

1/2 cup slivered fresh basil leaves

2 cups thick-and-chunky-style pasta sauce

1/4 to 1/2 teaspoon dried red pepper flakes (optional)

1/2 cup heavy cream

1/2 pound peeled and deveined medium or small shrimp

Salt and pepper to taste

1. Pour the water into a large pot, salt lightly, and cover. Bring to a boil over high heat. Add the ravioli, stir to separate, and cook according to the directions on the package, stirring gently, until *al dente*. About 1 minute before the ravioli are done, stir in the peas. Drain the peas and ravioli in a colander and return to the pot. Cover to keep warm.

2. While the ravioli cook, sliver enough fresh basil leaves to measure 1/2 cup.

3. In a large nonstick skillet, bring the pasta sauce and dried red pepper flakes, if using, to a boil over medium-high heat. Reduce the heat and simmer for 2 minutes. Stir in the cream, return to a simmer, and cook for 1 minute.

4. Stir in the shrimp. Simmer for 2 to 3 minutes, stirring often, until the shrimp are pink and just opaque in the thickest part. Remove the pan from the heat. Do not overcook the shrimp.

5. Stir the basil into the sauce and season with salt and pepper. Pour the sauce over the ravioli and peas and toss to coat. Cover to keep warm.

step 2

assemble the **antipasto salad**

1 jar (6 1/2 ounces) marinated artichoke hearts

1 jar (7 ounces) roasted red peppers

1/2 cup marinated olives

1/2 cup sliced celery

1 tablespoon balsamic vinegar

3 cups prewashed colorful mixed salad greens

1. Drain the artichoke hearts, reserving 1 tablespoon of the oil. Put in a salad bowl. Drain the roasted peppers and cut them into 1-inch pieces. Add them to the artichokes.

2. Add the olives, celery, vinegar, and reserved marinating oil. Toss. Mound the greens on top. Place the bowl on the table, with 4 salad plates.

step 3

serve

1. Serve the pasta in 4 pasta bowls.

2. Toss the salad at the table, and serve on the salad plates.

3. When ready for dessert, scoop the gelato into 4 dessert bowls. Serve.

Ravioli with Shrimp, Peas, and Tomato Cream
Single serving is 1/4 of total recipe

CALORIES 516; PROTEIN 28g; CARBS 54g; TOTAL FAT 22g; SAT FAT 13g; CHOLESTEROL 155mg; SODIUM 1267mg; FIBER 7g

salsa pasta olé

green salad with chili vinaigrette

honeyed cantaloupe with blueberries

menu gameplan

shopping list

Refrigerated cheese tortelloni

Fully cooked chicken or turkey sausage

Mild chunky salsa

Pre-shredded Monterey Jack cheese

Red pepper slices (from the salad bar)

Prewashed baby salad greens with fresh herbs

Pumpkin seeds, shelled

Lemon (for juice)

Fresh blueberries

Cantaloupe cubes (from the produce department)

from your pantry

Salt

Grated Parmesan cheese

Vinaigrette dressing, store-bought

Chili powder

Ground cumin

Honey

Ground cinnamon

serves 4

beforeyoustart

Bring a large pot of water, covered, to a boil over high heat to cook the pasta. Preheat the broiler.

step 1 make the **salsa pasta olé**

step 2 assemble the **green salad with chili vinaigrette**

step 3 prepare the **honeyed cantaloupe with blueberries**

step 4 **serve**

luckyforyou Fresh pasta, even filled fresh pasta, cooks very quickly.

"What to do with fresh cheese tortelloni besides tossing it with marinara sauce? How about a Mexican casserole with sausage, salsa, and cheese?"

—minutemeals' Chef Sarah

step 1

make the **salsa pasta olé**

4 quarts water

Salt to taste

2 packages (9 ounces each) refrigerated cheese tortelloni

1/2 pound fully cooked chicken or turkey sausage

1 jar (16 ounces) mild chunky salsa

1 cup pre-shredded Monterey Jack cheese

1/4 cup grated Parmesan cheese

1. Pour the water into a large pot, salt lightly, and cover. Bring to a boil over high heat. Add the tortelloni, stir to separate, and cook according to the directions on the package. Drain in a colander.

2. Preheat the broiler. Meanwhile, slice the sausage into thin rounds.

3. In a medium nonstick skillet, cook the sausage over medium-high heat, stirring frequently, until it begins to brown lightly, about 3 minutes. Remove the skillet from the heat.

4. In the same pot used to cook the pasta, bring the salsa to a boil. Remove the pot from the heat; stir in the tortelloni, 1/2 cup of the Monterey Jack cheese, and the sausage until well combined.

5. Spoon the pasta into a metal broiler-proof 2 1/2-quart casserole. Top with the remaining 1/2 cup Monterey Jack cheese and the Parmesan. Broil 5 to 6 inches from the heat for 2 to 3 minutes, until browned on the top and bubbly.

step 2

assemble the **green salad with chili vinaigrette**

1/2 cup red pepper slices

2 tablespoons store-bought vinaigrette dressing

1/4 teaspoon chili powder

1/4 teaspoon ground cumin

1 bag (5 ounces) prewashed baby salad greens with fresh herbs

2 tablespoons raw or toasted shelled pumpkin seeds

1. Coarsely chop the pepper slices.

2. In a large bowl, stir the chopped pepper, vinaigrette, chili powder, and cumin until blended. Add the salad greens and pumpkin seeds. Place the bowl on the table, with 4 salad plates.

step 3

prepare the **honeyed cantaloupe with blueberries**

1 tablespoon fresh lemon juice (1 lemon)

2 tablespoons honey

Pinch of ground cinnamon

1 cup fresh blueberries

3 cups precut cantaloupe cubes

1. Squeeze 1 tablespoon lemon juice into a medium bowl. Add the honey and cinnamon and whisk until blended.

2. Pick over the blueberries, rinse, and drain well.

3. Add the blueberries and cantaloupe to the lemon honey and toss gently to coat.

step 4

serve

1. Place the pasta casserole on the table, and serve in 4 pasta bowls.

2. Toss the salad at the table, and serve on the salad plates.

3. When ready for dessert, spoon the fruit with some of the honey syrup into 4 dessert dishes, and serve.

Salsa Pasta Olé
Single serving is 1/4 of total recipe

CALORIES 629; PROTEIN 37g; CARBS 66g; TOTAL FAT 23g; SAT FAT 14g; CHOLESTEROL 94mg; SODIUM 1905mg; FIBER 4g

☆ chinese chicken soup

crispy chinese noodles
peas and carrot salad
honey almond gelato

menu
gameplan

serves 4

beforeyoustart

Bring the chicken broth and water to a boil in a 5- to 6-quart saucepan or Dutch oven, covered.

step 1 prepare the **peas and carrot salad**

step 2 cook the **chinese chicken soup**

step 3 **serve**

shopping list

Small red onion

Frozen tiny peas

Gingerroot

Frozen gyoza or potstickers

Skinless boneless chicken breasts, thin-sliced

Precut Oriental stir-fry vegetables, fresh or frozen

Wide crispy Chinese noodles

Duck sauce

Honey almond gelato

from the salad bar

Stringed snow peas

Pre-shredded carrots (or from the produce department)

Chopped scallions

from your pantry

Rice vinegar

Vegetable oil

Salt and pepper

Fat-free reduced-sodium chicken broth

Lite soy sauce

Toasted sesame oil

headsup

When you use the same cutting board to cut both vegetables and meat, cut the vegetables up first. That way you won't have to wash the cutting board in between.

step 1

prepare the **peas and carrot salad**

1 tablespoon chopped red onion (1 small red onion)

1 cup stringed snow peas

1 cup pre-shredded carrots

1/2 cup frozen tiny peas

2 tablespoons rice vinegar

2 teaspoons vegetable oil

Salt and pepper to taste

1. Finely chop enough onion to measure 1 tablespoon. Stack the snow peas and slice them lengthwise into thin strips.

2. In a medium microwave-safe bowl, combine the onion, snow peas, carrots, frozen peas, vinegar, vegetable oil, and salt and pepper. Microwave on High for 1 minute, stirring once, or until the peas are defrosted. Place the bowl on the table, with 4 salad plates.

step 2

cook the **chinese chicken soup**

3 cans (14 1/2 ounces each) fat-free reduced-sodium chicken broth

3/4 cup water

1 teaspoon grated fresh ginger (1/2-inch piece gingerroot)

2 tablespoons lite soy sauce

1 teaspoon toasted sesame oil

20 frozen gyoza or potstickers (1 1/4 pounds)

1/2 pound thin-sliced skinless boneless chicken breasts

4 cups fresh or thawed frozen precut Oriental stir-fry vegetables

1/4 cup chopped scallions

1. Pour the chicken broth and water into a 5- to 6-quart saucepan or Dutch oven, cover, and bring to a boil over high heat.

2. Finely grate the ginger to measure 1 teaspoon. Stir the ginger, soy sauce, sesame oil, and gyoza or potstickers into the boiling liquid. Cover and bring to a boil. Reduce the heat to medium and simmer, covered, for 5 minutes

3. While the soup simmers, slice the chicken breasts crosswise into 1/2-inch-wide strips.

4. Add the vegetables to the soup. Cover and return the mixture to a boil. Reduce the heat and simmer for 2 minutes, covered, or until the vegetables are tender. (Frozen vegetables will take 1 or 2 minutes longer to cook than fresh vegetables.)

5. Stir in the chicken strips and simmer for 1 minute, or until cooked through. Stir in the scallions and remove the pan from the heat.

step 3

serve

1. Place the crispy Chinese noodles in a basket or bowl and serve with 2 shallow bowls of duck sauce for dipping.

2. Ladle the soup into 4 deep soup bowls and serve.

3. Toss the salad at the table, on the salad plates and serve.

4. When ready for dessert, scoop the gelato into 4 dessert bowls and serve.

Chinese Chicken Soup
Single serving is 1/4 of total recipe

CALORIES 453; PROTEIN 33g; CARBS 42g; TOTAL FAT 17g; SAT FAT 5g; CHOLESTEROL 103mg; SODIUM 1731mg; FIBER 5g

shrimp, goat cheese, and roasted red pepper pizza

arugula, red onion, and black olive salad

pizzelle ice cream sandwiches

shopping list

Pillsbury® Refrigerated Pizza Crust

Precooked shrimp, peeled and deveined

Jarred roasted red peppers

Goat cheese

Arugula

Red onion

Kalamata olives, pitted

Coffee ice cream

M&M candies

Pizzelle cookies

from your pantry

Vegetable cooking spray

Garlic

Dried oregano

Vinaigrette dressing, store-bought

Salt and pepper

serves 4

beforeyoustart

Preheat the oven to 425°F to bake the pizza.

step	1	make the **pizza**
step	2	assemble the **salad**
step	3	prepare the **pizzelle ice cream sandwiches**
step	4	**serve**

luckyforyou

Precooked shelled shrimp are widely available and if you can't find them fresh, purchase them frozen. Thawing is quick. If you buy "cocktail" shrimp, remember that they often have the tail shells still attached. It will take time to remove them.

"There are so many different styles of goat cheese now. Use soft goat cheese here. For variety, try an herb- or pepper-flavored one."

—minutemeals' Chef Hillary

step 1
make the **shrimp, goat cheese, and roasted red pepper pizza**

Vegetable cooking spray

1 package (10 ounces) Pillsbury® Refrigerated Pizza Crust

1/2 pound precooked, peeled, and deveined shrimp

1 jar (7 ounces) roasted red peppers

2 garlic cloves

1 teaspoon dried oregano

1 log (4 ounces) goat cheese

1. Preheat the oven to 425°F. Spray a 12- × 8-inch jelly-roll pan with vegetable cooking spray. Unroll the pizza dough and fit it into the prepared pan. Bake for 6 minutes.

2. Cut the shrimp into 1/2-inch pieces. Drain and chop the roasted red peppers. Mince the garlic. Combine the shrimp, peppers, garlic, and oregano in a medium bowl.

3. Remove the pizza crust from the oven and spread the shrimp mixture over it. Crumble the goat cheese evenly over the pizza topping and bake for 6 to 8 minutes, until the topping is hot.

step 2
assemble the **arugula, red onion, and black olive salad**

2 bunches of arugula

1 small red onion

1/2 cup pitted kalamata olives

2 to 4 tablespoons store-bought vinaigrette dressing

Salt and pepper to taste

1. Stem the arugula, rinse well, and pat dry. Halve the red onion and thinly slice.

2. In a salad bowl, combine the arugula, red onion slices, olives, and dressing. Season with salt and pepper. Place the bowl on the table.

step 3
prepare the **pizzelle ice cream sandwiches**

1 pint coffee ice cream

1/2 cup chopped M&M candies

8 pizzelle cookies

1. Remove the ice cream from the freezer to soften slightly. Chop enough M&M's to measure 1/2 cup.

2. Place 4 pizzelle cookies on a serving platter and top each with a scoop of ice cream. Sprinkle with chopped M&Ms. Place 1 of the remaining pizzelle cookies on top. Place the ice cream sandwiches on a platter and freeze until serving time.

step 4
serve

1. Place the pizza on the table and cut it into squares with a pizza cutter or sharp knife. Serve on dinner plates.

2. Toss the salad at the table and serve it alongside the pizza.

3. When ready for dessert, serve the ice cream sandwiches directly from the freezer.

Shrimp, Goat Cheese, and Roasted Red Pepper Pizza
Single serving is 1/4 of total recipe
CALORIES 346; PROTEIN 24g; CARBS 36g; TOTAL FAT 11g; SAT FAT 6g; CHOLESTEROL 133mg; SODIUM 781mg; FIBER 1g

bacon and tomato pizzettes
antipasto salad
raspberry yogurt parfaits

shopping list

Precooked bacon slices

Red tomatoes

Yellow tomatoes

Kontos brand Pizza Parlor Crusts

Pre-shredded part-skim mozzarella

Prewashed spring or mixed greens

Assorted olives
(jarred or from the olive bar)

Low-fat raspberry yogurt

Fresh raspberries

Reduced-fat granola

from the salad bar

Marinated artichoke hearts

Marinated mushrooms

from your pantry

Olive oil

Freshly ground black pepper or dried red pepper flakes

Dried basil

serves 4

beforeyoustart
Preheat the oven to 500°F to bake the pizzettes.

step **1** make the **bacon and tomato pizzettes**

step **2** plate the **antipasto salad**

step **3** prepare the **raspberry yogurt parfaits**

step **4** **serve**

luckyforyou Precooked bacon, called for on the pizzettes, is a great time-saver. All you have to do before using the slices is reheat them—ideally in the microwave.

"There seems to be a belief that homemade pizza is difficult to make. Not when you use premade pizza crust. It's easy, and a treat."

—minutemeals' Chef Hillary

step 1

make the **bacon and tomato pizzettes**

- 8 precooked bacon slices
- 2 medium red tomatoes
- 2 medium yellow tomatoes
- 4 Kontos brand Pizza Parlor Crusts (from 14-ounce package)
- 1 tablespoon olive oil
- 1 cup pre-shredded part-skim mozzarella
- Freshly ground black pepper or dried red pepper flakes
- 1 teaspoon dried basil

1. Preheat the oven to 500°F.

2. Put the bacon slices on a paper plate. Microwave the bacon on High for 1 to 2 minutes, or until heated. Coarsely chop.

3. Rinse the tomatoes, pat dry, and slice 1/4 inch thick.

4. Place the pizza crusts on a large cookie sheet. Brush the crusts with the olive oil. Arrange slices of red and yellow tomatoes, alternating them, on the crusts. Sprinkle with the bacon, mozzarella, black pepper or dried red pepper flakes, and the basil. Bake for 6 to 8 minutes, or until heated through and the cheese is bubbly. Transfer 1 pizzette to each of 4 dinner plates.

step 2

plate the **antipasto salad**

- 1 bag (5 ounces) prewashed spring or mixed greens
- Marinated artichoke hearts for 4
- Marinated mushrooms for 4
- Assorted olives

Line a serving platter with the salad greens. Arrange the artichoke hearts, mushrooms, and olives on the serving platter. Drizzle with some of the marinating liquid from the artichokes and mushrooms. Place the platter on the table.

step 3

prepare the **raspberry yogurt parfaits**

- 2 containers (8 ounces each) low-fat raspberry yogurt
- 1/2 pint fresh raspberries
- 1/4 cup reduced-fat granola

Place a spoonful of the yogurt in the bottom of each of 4 wine glasses or dessert dishes. Top with raspberries, granola, and the remaining yogurt. Chill until serving time.

step 4

serve

1. Serve the pizzettes at once, with the antipasto salad alongside as an accompaniment.

2. When ready for dessert, serve the parfaits.

Bacon and Tomato Pizzettes
Single serving is 1/4 of total recipe

CALORIES 472; PROTEIN 22g; CARBS 61g; TOTAL FAT 18g; SAT FAT 7g; CHOLESTEROL 35mg; SODIUM 1009mg; FIBER 4g

southwestern hamburger pizza
crisp iceberg salads
banana splits

shopping list

Ground beef (80 to 85% lean)

Tomato pasta or pizza sauce

Frozen corn kernels

Chopped mild green chiles

Boboli pizza crust

Pre-shredded Monterey Jack cheese

Salsa

Iceberg lettuce

Tomato

Cucumber slices (from the salad bar)

French or Italian salad dressing

Strawberry or banana ice cream

Ripe bananas

Chopped walnuts

from your pantry

Vegetable cooking spray

Salt and pepper

Chocolate sauce or syrup

serves 4

beforeyoustart

Preheat the oven to 500°F to bake the pizza.

step **1** make the **southwestern hamburger pizza**

step **2** assemble the **crisp iceberg salads**

step **3** prepare the **banana splits**

step **4** **serve**

 The higher the fat content the better the flavor in ground beef. That said, 80 to 85% lean ground beef has enough fat to ensure good flavor in the hamburger topping here. You will still need to drain the cooked meat, however, to ensure a crisp pizza crust.

"Make the topping more Southwestern-tasting by stirring in fresh chopped cilantro and a squeeze of fresh lime juice at the end of cooking."

—minutemeals' Chef Hillary

step 1

make the **southwestern hamburger pizza**

Vegetable cooking spray

1 pound ground beef
(80 to 85% lean)

1 jar (10 ounces) tomato
pasta or pizza sauce

1 cup frozen corn kernels

1 can (4$\frac{1}{2}$ ounces) chopped
mild green chiles

Salt and pepper to taste

1 premade Boboli pizza crust
(10 ounces)

$\frac{1}{2}$ cup pre-shredded
Monterey Jack cheese

Prepared salsa for serving

1. Preheat the oven to 500°F.

2. Spray a large deep heavy skillet with vegetable cooking spray and heat over high heat. Crumble in the beef and cook, stirring often to break up the chunks, for 3 to 5 minutes, or until no longer pink. Drain in a colander and return to the pan. Add the pasta or pizza sauce, corn, green chiles, and salt and pepper. Bring to a simmer, reduce the heat slightly, and simmer for 2 to 3 minutes, or until slightly thickened.

3. Place the pizza crust on a large cookie sheet. Spoon the beef mixture onto the crust and sprinkle the Monterey Jack cheese over the top. Bake for 5 minutes, or until the cheese has melted and the filling is hot and bubbly.

step 2

assemble the **crisp iceberg salads**

1 large head iceberg lettuce

1 large tomato

1 cup cucumber slices

2 to 4 tablespoons store-bought
French or Italian salad dressing

1. Core the iceberg lettuce and quarter the head. Rinse the tomato, pat dry, and cut into 8 wedges.

2. Place a wedge of the iceberg in each of 4 salad bowls. Divide the tomatoes and cucumbers evenly among the bowls and drizzle each salad with dressing. Place the bowls on the table.

step 3

prepare the **banana splits**

1 pint strawberry or banana
ice cream

2 ripe large bananas

$\frac{1}{2}$ cup jarred chocolate sauce
or syrup

$\frac{1}{2}$ cup chopped walnuts

Remove the ice cream from the freezer to soften slightly.

step 4

serve

1. Cut the pizza into wedges. Serve on 4 dinner plates, with the salsa for adding at the table.

2. When ready for dessert, halve each of the bananas lengthwise. Place the pieces in 4 shallow dessert bowls or banana split dishes. Scoop ice cream over the bananas, pour chocolate sauce on top, and sprinkle walnuts over all. Serve at once.

Southwestern Hamburger Pizza
Single serving is $\frac{1}{4}$ of total recipe
CALORIES 524; PROTEIN 35g; CARBS 48g;
TOTAL FAT 20g; SAT FAT 9g; CHOLESTEROL 88mg;
SODIUM 1168mg; FIBER 4g

mini rigatoni
with beans and gazpacho sauce

italian salad with marinated mushrooms

cannoli or spumoni ice cream

menu gameplan

serves 4

beforeyoustart

Bring a large pot of water, covered, to a boil over high heat to cook the rigatoni.

step	1	make the **mini rigatoni with beans and gazpacho sauce**

step	2	assemble the **salad**

step	3	**serve**

shopping list

Mini rigatoni

Pinto beans

Red onion

Cucumber

Fresh parsley

Medium-hot thick-and-chunky salsa

No-salt-added tomato sauce

Marinated mushrooms (jarred or from the salad bar)

Prewashed Italian-blend salad greens

Balsamic vinaigrette dressing

Chunk of Parmesan cheese

Cannoli (from the bakery section) or spumoni ice cream

from your pantry

Salt

Red wine vinegar

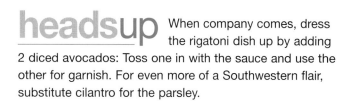

headsup When company comes, dress the rigatoni dish up by adding 2 diced avocados: Toss one in with the sauce and use the other for garnish. For even more of a Southwestern flair, substitute cilantro for the parsley.

"This is a great do-ahead menu for hot weather. Beat the heat by cooking in the morning, then refrigerate the components until serving time."

—minutemeals' Chef Paul

step 1

make the **mini rigatoni with beans and gazpacho sauce**

4 quarts water

Salt to taste

12 ounces mini rigatoni

1 can (15 ounces) pinto beans

1/2 red onion

for the gazpacho sauce

1 small cucumber

1/4 cup packed parsley leaves

1 cup prepared medium-hot thick-and-chunky salsa

1 can (8 ounces) no-salt-added tomato sauce

1 tablespoon red wine vinegar

1. Pour the water into a large pot, salt lightly, and cover. Bring to a boil over high heat. Add the rigatoni, stir to separate, and cook according to the directions on the package until *al dente*.

2. While the pasta is cooking, drain the beans in a large colander. Chop the onion and place it in the colander with the beans. Drain the rigatoni over the beans and onion in the colander. Rinse with cold water and drain well. Let stand while making the sauce.

3. Make the gazpacho sauce: Peel and coarsely chop the cucumber; place in a large serving bowl. Chop the parsley and add it to the bowl along with the salsa, tomato sauce, and vinegar. Stir to combine.

4. Add the rigatoni, bean, and onions to the sauce and toss well to coat.

step 2

assemble the **italian salad with marinated mushrooms**

8 ounces marinated mushrooms

2 to 3 tablespoons balsamic vinaigrette dressing

1 package (7 ounces) prewashed Italian-blend salad greens

Chunk of Parmesan cheese

1. Drain the mushrooms and cut them into quarters. Place in a salad bowl, along with the vinaigrette. Mound the greens on top. Do not toss until serving. Place the bowl on the table with 4 salad bowls.

2. Using a swivel-bladed peeler, shave 1/4 cup thin pieces off the chunk of Parmesan. Place in a bowl and put the bowl on the table.

step 3

serve

1. Serve the pasta in 4 pasta bowls.

2. Toss the salad at the table, and serve it in the salad bowls. Scatter the Parmesan shavings among the salad bowls and serve.

3. When ready for dessert, serve the cannoli or spumoni on dessert plates.

Mini Rigatoni with Beans and Gazpacho Sauce
Single serving is 1/4 of total recipe
CALORIES 421; PROTEIN 16g; CARBS 84g; TOTAL FAT 3g; SAT FAT 1g; CHOLESTEROL 0mg; SODIUM 617mg; FIBER 8g;

mexican tortilla pizzas

tex-mex broccoli slaw
mango sorbet with strawberries or cherries

serves 4

shopping list

Cilantro

Thick-and-chunky salsa

Broccoli slaw (bagged, from the produce department)

Flour tortillas (10-inch diameter)

Black beans

Chopped green chiles

Frozen or canned corn kernels

Pre-shredded Mexican mix cheese

Mango sorbet

Strawberries or cherries

from your pantry

Mild olive or vegetable oil

Cider vinegar

Sugar

Salt and pepper

Nonstick olive oil cooking spray

Ground cumin

beforeyoustart

Preheat the oven to 450°F to bake the pizzas.

step 1 make the **tex-mex broccoli slaw**

step 2 prepare the **mexican tortilla pizzas**

step 3 **serve**

 luckyforyou Tortillas now come in a wide variety of flavorings. You can add additional zip to your pizzas by simply substituting these for the called-for flour tortillas.

step 1

make the **tex-mex broccoli slaw**

3 tablespoons cilantro leaves

1/3 cup prepared thick-and-chunky salsa

2 tablespoons mild olive or vegetable oil

2 tablespoons cider vinegar

2 teaspoons sugar

1 package (12 ounces) broccoli slaw

Salt and pepper to taste

1. Chop the cilantro.

2. Combine the salsa, oil, vinegar, sugar, and cilantro in a large bowl. (If the salsa is very thick, mash it against the side of the bowl with the back of a spoon to liquefy it.)

3. Add the broccoli slaw and toss until evenly coated with the dressing. Season with salt and pepper. Place the bowl on the table.

step 2

prepare the **mexican tortilla pizzas**

4 large flour tortillas (10-inch diameter)

Nonstick olive oil cooking spray

1 cup prepared thick-and-chunky salsa

1 teaspoon ground cumin

2 tablespoons cilantro leaves

1 can (15 ounces) black beans

1 can (4 1/2 ounces) chopped green chiles

1 cup frozen or canned and drained corn kernels

1 1/2 cups pre-shredded Mexican mix cheese

1. Preheat the oven to 450°F.

2. Place the tortillas on 2 baking sheets. Spray the tops of the tortillas with nonstick olive oil cooking spray. Bake for 4 minutes, or until puffy.

3. Meanwhile, in a medium bowl, stir together the salsa, cumin, and cilantro. (If the salsa has a lot of liquid, drain it in a sieve before using.)

4. Drain the beans and green chiles in a colander. Add them to the bowl, along with the corn; stir to combine. Spoon the bean mixture on the tortillas, spreading in an even layer. Top each tortilla with some of the shredded cheese. Bake the pizzas for 5 to 6 minutes, or until the cheese is melted and the edges are golden brown.

step 3

serve

1. Place each pizza on a dinner plate and serve at once, with the slaw alongside.

2. When ready for dessert, scoop the sorbet into 4 dessert bowls and serve with either the strawberries or cherries.

Mexican Tortilla Pizzas
Single serving is 1/4 of total recipe

CALORIES 551; PROTEIN 24g; CARBS 70g; TOTAL FAT 19g; SAT FAT 9g; CHOLESTEROL 38mg; SODIUM 1488mg; FIBER 10g

drunken beans

grilled chicken and basil sausages

chocolate fondue with strawberries and cake

menu gameplan

serves 4

step 1 make the **drunken beans**

step 2 cook the **grilled chicken and basil sausages**

step 3 prepare the **chocolate fondue**

step 4 **serve**

shopping list

Diced tomatoes with roasted garlic

Kidney beans

Beer, nonalcoholic beer, apple juice, or chicken broth

Baked beans

Smoky barbecue sauce

Chicken and basil sausage links

Bittersweet or semisweet chocolate chips

Heavy cream

Angel food or pound cake (from the bakery)

Fancy strawberries, preferably with stems

from the salad bar

Green pepper slices

Red onion slices

from your pantry

Mild red pepper sauce, such as Frank's® Redhot® Cayenne Pepper Sauce

Pure vanilla extract

headsup

Since the chocolate fondue can be served over ice cream as well, you may want to double the recipe. Store the extra, airtight, in the refrigerator and warm in the microwave right before using.

"Even though you use canned beans, these drunken beans taste homemade. You'll find yourself serving them often, with all kinds of grilled meats and poultry."

—minutemeals' Chef Paul

step 1

make the **drunken beans**

1 cup green pepper slices

1/2 cup red onion slices

1 can (14.5 ounces) drained diced tomatoes with roasted garlic

1 can (15 ounces) rinsed and drained kidney beans

1/2 cup beer, nonalcoholic beer, apple juice, or chicken broth

1 can (16 ounces) baked beans

1/3 cup smoky barbecue sauce

2 tablespoons mild red pepper sauce

1. Chop the green pepper slices and red onion slices. Drain the tomatoes. Rinse and drain the kidney beans.

2. Place the beer, juice, or broth in a large skillet over medium-high heat. Add the chopped pepper and red onion and bring to boil. Cook for 3 minutes.

3. Add the drained tomatoes, baked beans, kidney beans, barbecue sauce, and pepper sauce. Cover and bring to a boil. Uncover, reduce the heat to medium-low, and simmer, stirring occasionally, for 6 minutes, or until thickened. Transfer the beans to a serving bowl.

step 2

cook the **grilled chicken and basil sausages**

1 pound chicken and basil sausage links

1. Heat a stovetop grill pan over medium heat. Or preheat the broiler.

2. Pierce 4 chicken and basil sausages with a fork and place in the heated grill pan or on the broiler-pan rack. Grill for 8 to 10 minutes, turning occasionally, until no longer pink in the center. With tongs, transfer the sausages to a serving plate.

step 3

prepare the **chocolate fondue with strawberries and cake**

6 ounces bittersweet or semisweet chocolate chips

1/3 cup heavy cream

1/2 teaspoon pure vanilla extract

2 slices of angel food or pound cake

12 large fancy strawberries, with stems attached

1. Place the chocolate chips in a medium microwave-safe bowl with the heavy cream. Microwave on High for 1 to 2 minutes, stirring

2 or 3 times during the cooking, until smooth. Stir in the vanilla.

2. Spoon the fondue into a small bowl and place in center of a serving platter.

3. Cut the cake into cubes. Arrange the cake and strawberries around the fondue, and cover with a slightly dampened paper towel.

step 4

serve

1. Place the drunken beans and grilled sausages on the table and let diners serve themselves.

2. When ready for dessert, place the fondue platter in the middle of the table, with 4 long-handled forks for dipping the cake pieces into the fondue. Use the long stems of the strawberries for dipping.

Drunken Beans
Single serving is 1/4 of total recipe

CALORIES 288; PROTEIN 12g; CARBS 56g;
TOTAL FAT 2g; SAT FAT 0g; CHOLESTEROL 3mg;
SODIUM 1362mg; FIBER 13g

ham- and rosemary-stuffed portobellos
buttered orzo
steamed cauliflower and carrots
turtle ice cream sundaes

menu
gameplan

shopping list

Portobello mushrooms

Baked ham, sliced

Scallions

Fresh rosemary

Grated Asiago or Parmesan cheese

Orzo

Cauliflower florets

Presliced carrots (from the salad bar or produce department)

Caramel sundae sauce

Chocolate chips

Pecan pieces

Ice cream

from your pantry

Olive oil

Garlic

Whole-wheat or mixed grain bread

Salt and pepper

Butter

serves 4

beforeyoustart
Preheat the oven to 425°F.
Bring 2 quarts water to a boil.

step 1 make the **ham- and rosemary-stuffed portobellos**

step 2 cook the **buttered orzo**

step 3 prepare the **steamed cauliflower and carrots**

step 4 make the **turtle sundae sauce**

step 5 **serve**

headsup
If you have a mini processor, use it to make quick work of the stuffing. Chop the garlic and rosemary in it. Cut the scallions into 2-inch lengths, then with on/off pulses chop them in it too.

"Stuffed mushrooms, a popular appetizer that can take so long to prepare, become a satisfying main course with very little effort when you use portobellos."

—minutemeals' Chef Paul

step 1

make the **ham- and rosemary-stuffed portobellos**

4 portobello mushrooms (about 1 pound)

2 tablespoons olive oil

6 ounces sliced baked ham

1 garlic clove

3 scallions

1 tablespoon chopped fresh rosemary

2 slices of whole-wheat or mixed grain bread

1/3 cup grated Asiago or Parmesan cheese

1. Preheat the oven to 425°F. Line a jelly-roll pan with foil.

2. Stem the mushrooms and reserve for another use. Wipe the mushroom caps with paper towels. Brush the tops with 1 tablespoon of the olive oil. Place on foil-lined pan, cap side down. Bake for 6 minutes.

3. Meanwhile, dice the ham. Mince the garlic. Finely chop the scallions. Chop enough rosemary to measure 1 tablespoon.

4. Tear the bread into large pieces and place in a food processor; pulse to medium-sized crumbs and transfer to a medium bowl.

5. Add the ham, cheese, garlic, scallions, rosemary, and 2 tablespoons water; stir until combined. Spoon the stuffing mixture onto the mushroom caps, mounding it in the center and pressing down on it gently with your hands. Bake for 5 minutes, or until heated through. Drizzle the mushrooms with the remaining 1 tablespoon olive oil.

step 2

cook the **buttered orzo**

2 quarts water

Salt to taste

1 cup orzo

1 tablespoon butter

Pour the water into a medium saucepan, salt lightly, and cover. Bring to a boil over high heat. Add the orzo, stir, and cook according to the directions on the package until *al dente*. Drain well in a colander and return to the saucepan. Add the butter and stir until melted. Cover to keep warm.

step 3

prepare the **steamed cauliflower and carrots**

8 ounces cauliflower florets

8 ounces presliced carrots

1. Pour 1 inch water into a large saucepan, cover, and bring to a boil over high heat.

2. Arrange the cauliflower and carrots in a steamer basket. When the water boils, carefully add the basket to the pan, cover, and steam until the vegetables are tender, for 5 to 7 minutes. Transfer the vegetables to a serving bowl and keep warm, covered.

step 4

prepare the **turtle sundae sauce**

3/4 cup jarred caramel sundae sauce

1/4 cup chocolate chips

1/3 cup pecan pieces

1 pint ice cream of choice

1. Pour the caramel sauce into a 2-cup microwave-safe measure. Add the chocolate chips and pecans.

2. Remove the ice cream from the freezer to soften slightly.

step 5

serve

1. Transfer a stuffed mushroom to each of 4 dinner plates and spoon a serving of the orzo alongside. Serve with the steamed vegetables.

2. When ready for dessert, scoop the ice cream into 4 dessert dishes. Microwave the sauce on High for 30 to 60 seconds, or just until heated through. Spoon the turtle sauce over the ice cream and serve the sundaes at once.

Ham- and Rosemary-Stuffed Portobellos
Single serving is 1/4 of total recipe

CALORIES 215; PROTEIN 13g; CARBS 13g; TOTAL FAT 11g; SAT FAT 3g; CHOLESTEROL 32mg; SODIUM 587mg; FIBER 3g

portobello "baked" pasta

spinach and radicchio with creamy garlic dressing

peach coupes with crumbled amaretti

shopping list

Macaroni

Marinara sauce

Portobello mushrooms

Pre-chopped garlic

Pre-shredded quick-melt mozzarella

Radicchio

Iceberg lettuce

Cherry tomatoes (from the salad bar)

Prewashed baby spinach

Creamy garlic dressing

Amaretti cookies

Peach halves in light syrup

Instant whipped cream

from your pantry

Salt and pepper

Olive oil

Dried red pepper flakes

Grated Parmesan cheese

serves 4

beforeyoustart

Bring a large pot of water, covered, to a boil over high heat to cook the pasta.

step 1 make the **portobello "baked" pasta**

step 2 assemble the **salad**

step 3 assemble the **peach coupes with crumbled amaretti**

step 4 **serve**

 **headsup** Adding mushrooms, garlic, and red pepper flakes to an inexpensive marinara sauce quickly adds flavor and heartiness. If you have some handy, toss in 1/4 cup of fresh chopped basil or prepared pesto to boost the flavor even more.

"This pasta is every bit as tasty as the baked version, but can be prepared and on the table in less than half the time."

—minutemeals' Chef Paul

step 1

make the **portobello "baked" pasta**

4 quarts water

Salt to taste

1 pound macaroni

1 jar (26 ounces) marinara sauce

3 portobello mushrooms (about 3/4 pound)

1 tablespoon olive oil

2 teaspoons pre-chopped garlic

1/4 teaspoon dried red pepper flakes

1 1/4 cups pre-shredded quick-melt mozzarella

1/3 cup grated Parmesan cheese

1. Pour the water into a large pot, salt lightly, and cover. Bring to a boil over high heat. Add the macaroni, stir, and cook according to the directions on package until just tender. Drain well in a colander and return to the pan. Stir in the marinara sauce.

2. Meanwhile, wipe the mushrooms with paper towels. Slice the mushroom caps in half and cut crosswise into 1-inch pieces.

3. Preheat the broiler.

4. Heat the olive oil in a large nonstick skillet over medium-high heat. Add the mushrooms and cook, stirring occasionally, for 4 minutes. Add the garlic and red pepper flakes and cook, stirring, for 30 seconds, until tender and lightly browned. Add the mushroom mixture to the sauced macaroni and toss to combine.

5. Spoon the pasta into a metal or broiler-proof 12- × 8-inch baking dish. Sprinkle the mozzarella and Parmesan on the top. Broil 4 to 6 inches from the heat for 2 to 3 minutes, just until the cheese is melted.

step 2

assemble the **spinach and radicchio with creamy garlic dressing**

1/2 head radicchio

1/2 head iceberg lettuce

1 cup cherry tomatoes

1 bag (5 ounces) prewashed baby spinach

1/4 cup store-bought creamy garlic dressing

Salt and pepper to taste

Cut out the core and slice the radicchio. Break the iceberg lettuce into bite-size pieces. Rinse the cherry tomatoes and pat dry. Place all in a large salad bowl with the remaining ingredients; do not toss until serving time. Place the bowl on the table.

step 3

assemble the **peach coupes with crumbled amaretti**

10 amaretti cookies

1 can (15 ounces) chilled peach halves in light syrup

Instant whipped cream

1. Place the amaretti cookies in a plastic bag, close the bag, and with a rolling pin coarsely crush them.

2. Spoon the peaches with a little of their syrup into 4 dessert dishes. Chill until serving time.

step 4

serve

1. Place the baked pasta on the table and serve directly from the baking dish.

2. Toss the salad at the table, and serve it alongside the pasta.

3. When ready for dessert, top the peaches with whipped cream, then sprinkle each serving with the crumbled amaretti. Serve.

Portobello "Baked" Pasta
Single serving is 1/4 of total recipe
CALORIES 838; PROTEIN 43g; CARBS 120g; TOTAL FAT 18g; SAT FAT 7g; CHOLESTEROL 34mg; SODIUM 1066mg; FIBER 9g

☆ focaccia
with portobellos and blue cheese

mixed vegetable juice

olive and chickpea salad

orange sorbet with grated chocolate

shopping list

Prebaked focaccia
(Italian flat bread)

Portobello mushroom caps

Shallots

Pre-chopped garlic

Crumbled Gorgonzola or
blue cheese

Pre-shredded mozzarella

Chickpeas

Brine-cured olives, pitted

Fresh basil leaves or parsley

Orange sorbet

Bittersweet chocolate

Vegetable juice (1 quart)

Lime

from your pantry

Olive oil

Dried thyme

Dry sherry or apple juice

Vinaigrette dressing,
store-bought or homemade

Pepper

serves 4

beforeyoustart

Preheat the oven to 450°F to bake
the focaccia.

step **1** bake the **focaccia**

step **2** assemble the **olive and chickpea salad**

step **3** prepare the **orange sorbet with grated chocolate**

step **4** serve

headsup
Focaccia is a popular flat
bread that can be found in
most supermarket bakeries. You can also use another
Italian flat bread, *ciabatta,* or a prebaked pizza crust, or
even a small loaf of Italian bread. Split the regular Italian
loaf in half horizontally and place, cut sides up, on the
baking sheet, then proceed as directed.

"This vegetarian menu is filling and hearty and will satisfy the hungriest of families."

—minutemeals' Chef Paul

step 1

bake the **focaccia with portobellos and blue cheese**

- 1 small focaccia bread (12 ounces)
- 4 medium portobello mushroom caps (about 1 pound)
- 4 shallots, thinly sliced
- 2 tablespoons olive oil
- 1 teaspoon pre-chopped garlic
- 1/2 teaspoon dried thyme
- 3 tablespoons dry sherry or apple juice
- 1/2 cup crumbled Gorgonzola or blue cheese
- 1 cup pre-shredded mozzarella

1. Preheat the oven to 450°F. Place the focaccia on a baking sheet.

2. Wipe the portobello mushroom caps with a damp paper towel. Cut the caps in half and slice crosswise. Thinly slice the shallots.

3. Heat the olive oil in a large nonstick skillet over medium-high heat. Add the mushrooms and cook, stirring occasionally, for 5 minutes.

4. Add the shallots, garlic, thyme, and sherry and cook for 2 minutes, or until the liquid has evaporated and the mushrooms are tender.

5. Remove the pan from the heat and stir in the Gorgonzola. Spoon the mixture evenly over the focaccia and sprinkle on the mozzarella. Bake for 3 to 5 minutes, or until the cheese is melted and the bread is warmed.

step 2

assemble the **olive and chickpea salad**

- 1 shallot or white part of 2 scallions
- 1 can (19 ounces) chickpeas
- 1/2 cup brine-cured pitted olives
- 3 tablespoons vinaigrette dressing
- Pepper to taste
- 1/4 cup loosely packed basil leaves or chopped fresh parsley

1. Chop the shallot or white part of scallions and place in a medium bowl.

2. Rinse and drain the chickpeas. Slice the olives. Add the chickpeas, olives, and vinaigrette to the bowl and toss to combine. Season with pepper.

3. Thinly slice enough basil leaves or chop enough parsley to measure 1/4 cup and scatter over the salad; do not toss until serving time.

step 3

prepare the **orange sorbet with grated chocolate**

- 1 pint orange sorbet
- 1 bar bittersweet chocolate

1. Remove the sorbet from the freezer to soften slightly.

2. Grate about 1/4 cup of the chocolate.

step 4

serve

1. Pour the vegetable juice into 4 tall glasses. Cut the lime into 4 wedges and garnish each glass with a wedge. Place the glasses on the table.

2. Slide the focaccia onto a cutting board and with a sharp knife cut it into 4- × 2-inch rectangles. Serve from the cutting board.

3. Toss the salad at the table and serve alongside the focaccia.

4. When ready for dessert, scoop the sorbet into 4 dessert bowls and sprinkle each with grated chocolate. Serve, with the remaining bittersweet chocolate bar, broken into bits, if desired.

Focaccia with Portobellos and Blue Cheese
Single serving is 1/4 of total recipe

CALORIES 475; PROTEIN 16g; CARBS 50g;
TOTAL FAT 22g; SAT FAT 9g; CHOLESTEROL 35mg;
SODIUM 655mg; FIBER 3g

minute
3 ways

cheese, eggs, and meat substitute menus

meals

to dinner

veggie quesadillas
orange and avocado salad
strawberry sorbet

menu gameplan

serves 4

shopping list

Navel orange

Firm-ripe avocado

Marinated olives, pitted

Prewashed mixed
salad greens

Zucchini

Canned or frozen corn kernels

Flour tortillas (6- to 7-inch
diameter)

Pre-shredded Mexican
cheese blend

Salsa

Strawberry sorbet

from the salad bar

Green pepper slices

Red onion slices

from your pantry

Olive oil

Red wine vinegar

Salt and pepper

Chili powder

beforeyoustart

Preheat the oven to 425°F to bake
the quesadillas.

step 1 assemble the **orange
and avocado salad**

step 2 make the **veggie
quesadillas**

step 3 **serve**

luckyforyou Blended shredded cheeses
are available in convenient
resealable bags. Mexican cheese blend is a mixture of
4 different cheeses. There are also blends called "taco,"
which have seasonings added to the shredded cheeses.

"Tortillas filled with vegetables and melted cheeses go great with this avocado, orange, and olive salad. It may sound unusual but the flavors blend well."

—minutemeals' Chef Sarah

step 1

assemble the **orange and avocado salad**

1 navel orange

1 firm-ripe avocado

$1/3$ cup pitted marinated olives

1 tablespoon olive oil

1 tablespoon red wine vinegar

Salt and pepper to taste

3 cups prewashed mixed salad greens

1. With a sharp knife, remove the peel and white membrane from the orange. Quarter the orange lengthwise and slice. Pit, peel, and dice the avocado. Coarsely chop the olives.

2. In a salad bowl, combine the orange slices, avocado, olives, oil, vinegar, and salt and pepper. Mound the salad greens on top; do not toss until serving time. Place the bowl on the table.

step 2

make the **veggie quesadillas**

1 cup green pepper slices

$1/2$ cup red onion slices

1 medium zucchini

$1/4$ cup water

1 cup drained canned or frozen corn kernels

1 teaspoon chili powder

Salt and pepper to taste

12 flour tortillas

1 bag (8 ounces) pre-shredded Mexican cheese blend

Prepared salsa for serving

1. Preheat the oven to 425°F.

2. Chop the pepper and onion slices. Trim and chop the zucchini.

3. In a large nonstick skillet, cook the chopped peppers and onion in the water over high heat until softened, about 2 minutes. Stir in the zucchini, corn, and chili powder. Cook for 2 to 3 minutes, or until the vegetables are tender-crisp and the water has evaporated. Remove the pan from the heat. Season with salt and pepper.

4. Arrange 4 tortillas in a single layer on a large baking sheet. Top with half of the vegetable mixture, spreading it to cover each tortilla. Sprinkle with half the cheese. Top each tortilla with another tortilla, the remaining vegetables, and the remaining cheese. Top with the remaining tortillas, pressing down on the layers. (You will have 4 quesadillas, each with 3 tortillas and filling.) Bake for 5 minutes, or until the filling is hot and the cheese melts.

step 3

serve

1. Transfer 1 quesadilla to each of 4 dinner plates and cut into wedges. Serve with salsa on the side.

2. Toss the salad at the table and serve it alongside the quesadillas, or on 4 separate salad plates.

3. When ready for dessert, scoop the sorbet into 4 dessert bowls and serve.

Veggie Quesadillas
Single serving is $1/4$ of total recipe
CALORIES 535; PROTEIN 25g; CARBS 52g;
TOTAL FAT 27g; SAT FAT 11g; CHOLESTEROL 51mg;
SODIUM 1132mg; FIBER 3g

new orleans muffulettas

deli potato or
macaroni salad

praline sundaes

shopping list

Jarred marinated artichoke
salad

Sliced celery
(from the salad bar)

Crusty sandwich rolls

Baked ham, sliced

Provolone cheese, sliced

Hard salami, sliced

Potato or macaroni salad
(from the deli counter)

Butter pecan ice cream

Caramel or butterscotch
ice cream topping

Chopped pecans

from your pantry

Garlic

Dried oregano

serves 4

beforeyoustart
Place 4 dessert bowls in the freezer.

step **1** make the **new orleans muffulettas**

step **2** plate the **deli potato or macaroni salad**

step **3** prepare the **praline sundaes**

step **4** **serve**

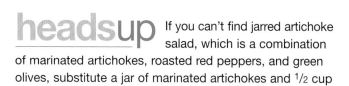 If you can't find jarred artichoke
salad, which is a combination
of marinated artichokes, roasted red peppers, and green
olives, substitute a jar of marinated artichokes and $1/2$ cup
pitted sliced pimiento-stuffed green olives.

"Who can resist a sandwich that is unique to New Orleans that's made with cold cuts, provolone, and a special artichoke-olive salad?"

—minutemeals' Chef Sarah

step 1

make the **new orleans muffulettas**

1 jar (12 ounces) marinated artichoke salad

1/2 cup sliced celery

1 large garlic clove

1/4 teaspoon dried oregano

4 large crusty sandwich rolls

1/2 pound sliced baked ham

1/2 pound sliced provolone cheese

1/4 pound sliced hard salami

1. Drain the artichoke salad, reserving 1 tablespoon of the marinade. Chop the artichoke salad and celery. Mince the garlic.

2. In a medium bowl, stir together the artichoke mixture, celery, garlic, oregano, and reserved marinade until combined.

3. Split the sandwich rolls in half horizontally. Lay the rolls cut sides up on the work surface. Cover the cut sides with artichoke salad.

Arrange ham, cheese, and salami on the bottom halves, dividing them equally. Cover each bottom half with a top half, pressing down lightly on the bread. Cut each sandwich in half, and secure the halves with toothpicks. (The sandwiches can also be served warm: Wrap each whole sandwich in foil and heat in a 350°F oven about 15 minutes, until the cheese melts.)

step 2

plate the **deli potato or macaroni salad**

Potato or macaroni salad for 4

Spoon the salad into a serving bowl. Place the bowl on the table.

step 3

prepare the **praline sundaes**

1 pint butter pecan ice cream

1/2 cup caramel or butterscotch ice cream topping

1/4 cup chopped pecans

1. Scoop ice cream into the 4 chilled dessert bowls and return to the freezer.

2. In a microwave-safe bowl, heat the ice cream topping on High until warm, about 1 minute. Keep warm.

step 4

serve

1. Place 1 sandwich on each of 4 dinner plates, and serve with the potato or macaroni salad.

2. When ready for dessert, rewarm the praline sauce, if necessary. Spoon some of the sauce over each serving of ice cream, sprinkle with pecans, and serve.

New Orleans Muffulettas
Single serving is 1/4 of total recipe
CALORIES 889; PROTEIN 43g; CARBS 76g;
TOTAL FAT 47g; SAT FAT 16g; CHOLESTEROL 90mg;
SODIUM 3148mg; FIBER 6g

cheddar cheese fondue

apple-pecan slaw
free-form strawberry tarts

menu
gameplan

serves 4

step 1 assemble the **free-form strawberry tarts**

step 2 make the **apple-pecan slaw**

step 3 make the **cheddar cheese fondue**

step 4 **serve**

shopping list

Strawberries

Raspberry jam

Heavy cream

Sugar cookies

Apple

Red onion

Pre-shredded coleslaw mix
(from the produce department)

Chopped pecans

Red wine vinegar and oil
salad dressing

French bread

Ale or beer

Pre-shredded sharp
Cheddar cheese

from the salad bar

Cherry tomatoes

Broccoli florets
(or from the produce
department)

from your pantry

Sugar

Salt and pepper

All-purpose flour

Dry mustard

headsup Be sure to let each handful of cheese melt before adding the next, so that the fondue remains smooth.

"Fondue is making a comeback. Classic Swiss fondue is made from Gruyère and kirsch. Here Cheddar and ale make it more of an English fondue."

—minutemeals' Chef Sarah

step 1

assemble the **free-form strawberry tarts**

- 1 pint strawberries
- 2 tablespoons sugar
- 1 tablespoon raspberry jam
- 1/2 cup heavy cream
- 4 large sugar cookies

1. Rinse the strawberries, hull, and slice them into a medium bowl. Add the sugar and toss.

2. In another medium bowl, beat the jam and heavy cream with an electric mixer on high speed until soft peaks form. Refrigerate.

3. Place 1 sugar cookie on each of 4 dessert plates.

step 2

make the **apple-pecan slaw**

- 1 apple
- 1 small red onion
- 2 cups pre-shredded coleslaw mix
- 2 tablespoons chopped pecans
- 2 to 3 tablespoons red wine vinegar and oil salad dressing
- Salt and pepper to taste

1. Quarter, core, and thinly slice the apple. Thinly slice enough red onion to measure 2 tablespoons.

2. In a medium bowl, combine the apple, red onion, coleslaw mix, pecans, and dressing. Toss to combine and season with salt and pepper. Place the bowl on the table with 4 salad plates.

step 3

make the **cheddar cheese fondue**

- 1 loaf crusty French bread
- 1 cup stemmed cherry tomatoes
- 2 cups small broccoli florets
- 1 cup ale or beer
- 4 cups pre-shredded sharp Cheddar cheese (1 pound)
- 1 1/2 tablespoons all-purpose flour
- 1 teaspoon dry mustard

1. Cut enough French bread into 1-inch cubes to measure 4 cups. Rinse the cherry tomatoes, stem if necessary, and pat dry. Arrange the broccoli florets, bread cubes, and cherry tomatoes on a large serving platter.

2. In a medium saucepan, heat the ale over low heat until it comes to a simmer.

3. In a medium bowl, toss together the Cheddar, flour, and mustard. Add a handful of cheese mixture to the saucepan and stir until totally melted. Repeat, adding the cheese mixture a handful at a time and stirring each time until completely melted. Do not boil.

4. Pour into a fondue pot and set over a flame to keep warm.

step 4

serve

1. Place the fondue on the table and serve warm with the vegetables and bread as dippers.

2. Serve the coleslaw on the salad plates.

3. When ready for dessert, spoon some of the sugared strawberries over each sugar cookie and top with the whipped cream. Serve, with the remaining whipped cream.

Cheddar Cheese Fondue
Single serving is 1/4 of total recipe
CALORIES 683; PROTEIN 36g; CARBS 45g;
TOTAL FAT 40g; SAT FAT 24g; CHOLESTEROL 119mg;
SODIUM 1146mg; FIBER 4g

giant omelette
parmesan toasts
lime-marinated melon

menu
gameplan

serves 4

beforeyoustart

Preheat the oven to 400°F.

step 1 prepare the **lime-marinated melon**

step 2 make the **parmesan toasts**

step 3 make the **giant omelette**

step 4 **serve**

shopping list

Seasonal melon cubes
(from the produce department)
or canned mandarin oranges

Limes (for juice)

Crusty Italian bread

Plum tomatoes

Prewashed spinach leaves

Pre-shredded mozzarella

Fresh basil

from your pantry

Sugar

Olive oil

Grated Parmesan cheese

Eggs

Salt and pepper

Butter

headsup   A large nonstick skillet really
works here to prevent the
eggs from sticking, making the transfer of the finished
omelette to the serving platter a whole lot easier.

"There's something comforting about savory eggs and toast for dinner. And when people are hungry, an omelette can be on the table in minutes."

—minutemeals' Chef Sarah

step 1

prepare the **lime-marinated melon**

4 cups cubed seasonal melon or canned mandarin oranges

2 tablespoons sugar

2 tablespoons fresh lime juice (2 limes)

In a medium bowl, toss the melon, sugar, and lime juice. Cover and refrigerate until serving. If using mandarin oranges, drain, divide among 4 dessert bowls, and refrigerate until serving time.

step 2

make the **parmesan toasts**

1/2 loaf crusty Italian bread

2 tablespoons olive oil

2 tablespoons grated Parmesan cheese

1. Preheat the oven to 400°F.

2. Cut the bread in half horizontally. Brush the cut sides with the olive oil and sprinkle with the Parmesan. Cut each half into 4 pieces and place them on a cookie sheet. Bake for 8 to 10 minutes, until toasted.

step 3

make the **giant omelette**

2 large plum tomatoes

8 large eggs

Salt and pepper to taste

2 tablespoons butter

1/4 cup grated Parmesan cheese

11/2 cups packed prewashed spinach leaves

1 cup pre-shredded mozzarella

1/2 cup lightly packed fresh basil leaves

1. Thinly slice the tomatoes.

2. Break the eggs into a medium bowl and beat them together lightly with a whisk. Season with salt and pepper.

3. In a large (12-inch) nonstick skillet, melt the butter over medium-high heat. Add the beaten eggs to the skillet; reduce the heat to low. Cook the eggs, lifting them with a spatula at the edges when set, tilting the skillet to let uncooked egg run underneath. When the eggs are set, but with a layer of unset moist egg on top, arrange the tomatoes, Parmesan, spinach, and mozzarella on top.

4. Stack the basil and tear into pieces. Sprinkle the basil over the mozzarella. Cover the skillet and cook, shaking the pan occasionally, about 4 minutes, or until the cheese melts.

5. Remove the skillet from the heat. With a spatula, loosen the eggs at the bottom of the pan, then slide the omelette onto a serving platter.

step 4

serve

1. Cut the omelette into 4 wedges and place a wedge on each of 4 dinner plates. Divide the Parmesan toasts among the plates. Serve.

2. When ready for dessert, divide the melon and lime marinade among 4 small bowls and serve.

Giant Omelette
Single serving is 1/4 of total recipe
CALORIES 303; PROTEIN 20g; CARBS 4g; TOTAL FAT 23g; SAT FAT 11g; CHOLESTEROL 465mg; SODIUM 409mg; FIBER 1g

huevos rancheros

cumin-scented beans
mashed avocado
orange-dipped strawberries

menu gameplan

shopping list

Strawberries

Orange (for zest and juice)

Pinto beans, or garbanzo, black, or white beans

Ripe avocado

Lime (for juice)

Diced tomatoes and mild green chiles

Mild salsa

Corn or flour tortillas (6-inch diameter)

Pre-shredded Monterey Jack cheese

from your pantry

Confectioners' sugar

Ground cumin

Hot pepper sauce

Salt and pepper

Vegetable oil

Eggs

serves 4

step 1   prepare the **orange-dipped strawberries**

step 2   heat the **cumin-scented beans**

step 3   prepare the **mashed avocado**

step 4   make the **huevos rancheros**

step 5   **serve**

headsup
If you have hearty eaters, cook 2 eggs per person: Fry the eggs 4 at a time. Remember to undercook the eggs slightly as they will continue to cook a bit while the cheese melts.

"These eggs with cheese and tomato sauce on tortillas are served in Mexico for breakfast, but they make a wonderful dinner that's quick to prepare."

—minutemeals' Chef Sarah

step 1

prepare the **orange-dipped strawberries**

1½ pints strawberries

1 orange

¼ cup confectioners' sugar

1. Rinse and dry the strawberries; place in a serving bowl.

2. Rinse the orange and with a grater or lemon zester remove 1 teaspoon zest. In a small bowl, combine the zest and confectioners' sugar.

3. Squeeze the orange and divide the juice among 4 small cups.

step 2

heat the **cumin-scented beans**

1 can (15 ounces) pinto beans

1 teaspoon ground cumin

3/4 teaspoon hot pepper sauce

Salt and pepper to taste

1. Drain and rinse beans.

2. In a medium saucepan, combine the beans, cumin, and hot pepper sauce. Season with salt and pepper. Bring to a boil, reduce heat to low, and cook for 5 minutes, or until heated through.

step 3

prepare the **mashed avocado**

1 large ripe avocado

1 tablespoon fresh lime juice (1 lime)

Salt and pepper to taste

1. Cut the avocado in half and remove the pit. With a spoon remove the avocado from the peel and place in a medium bowl. Mash lightly with a fork, leaving some chunks.

2. Squeeze about 1 tablespoon lime juice into the avocado and season with salt and pepper. Stir to combine. Place the bowl on the table.

step 4

make the **huevos rancheros**

1 can (10 ounces) diced tomatoes and mild green chiles

1/3 cup mild salsa, preferably garlic and cilantro flavored

2 tablespoons vegetable oil

4 corn or flour tortillas

4 large eggs

Salt and pepper to taste

3/4 cup pre-shredded Monterey Jack cheese

1. Drain the tomatoes and place in a medium saucepan. Stir in the salsa and bring to a boil over high heat. Reduce the heat to low and simmer the mixture while you cook the eggs.

2. In a large (12-inch) nonstick skillet, heat 1 tablespoon of the vegetable oil over medium-high heat. Add the tortillas, 1 at a time, and cook until softened and hot, about 15 seconds per side. Place 1 tortilla on each of 4 dinner plates.

3. Add the remaining 1 tablespoon vegetable oil to the skillet and reduce the heat to medium-low. Crack eggs into the skillet and cook until the whites begin to set, about 1 minute. Reduce the heat to low, cover the skillet, and cook until the yolks are done to the desired doneness, 2 to 3 minutes. Season with salt and pepper. Sprinkle the eggs with the cheese, remove the pan from the heat, cover, and let stand 1 minute or so to melt the cheese. Top each tortilla with an egg.

step 5

serve

1. Spoon the heated tomato sauce over each serving and add beans to each plate. Serve, with the mashed avocado as an accompaniment.

2. When ready for dessert, place the strawberries, orange sugar, and cups of orange juice on the table. To eat, dip a strawberry in the orange juice and then in the orange sugar.

Huevos Rancheros
Single serving is ¼ of total recipe
CALORIES 296; PROTEIN 14g; CARBS 18g;
TOTAL FAT 19g; SAT FAT 6g; CHOLESTEROL 244mg;
SODIUM 673mg; FIBER 3g

mu shu roll-ups

ginger-sesame broccoli
orange sorbet sandwiches

shopping list

Orange or lemon sorbet

Packaged large soft molasses cookies

Gingerroot

Broccoli florets
(from the salad bar or produce department)

Flour tortillas (10-inch diameter)

Shiitake mushrooms

Scallions

Pre-shredded coleslaw mix
(from the produce department)

Prepared garlic-and-ginger stir-fry sauce

from your pantry

Toasted sesame oil

Eggs

Vegetable oil

Hoisin sauce (optional)

serves 4

beforeyoustart

Preheat the oven to 350°F to heat the tortillas.

step **1** prepare the **orange sorbet sandwiches**

step **2** cook the **ginger-sesame broccoli**

step **3** make the **mu shu roll-ups**

step **4** **serve**

headsup To save time, you can use 2 cups presliced white button mushrooms instead of the shiitake mushrooms, but the extra minute or so that it takes to stem and slice the shiitakes is worth it for their more pronounced flavor. If mixed mushrooms are available at your market, use them.

"Softly scrambled eggs and crunchy stir-fried vegetables blended with a tasty sauce, all wrapped in a warm tortilla, make a winning combination."

—minutemeals' Chef Sarah

step 1

prepare the **orange sorbet sandwiches**

1 pint orange or lemon sorbet

8 packaged large soft molasses cookies

With scissors, cut down the side of the sorbet carton and remove the sorbet. With a knife, cut the sorbet crosswise into 4 slices. Place each slice between 2 cookies, place the cookies on a large plate, and freeze until serving time.

step 2

cook the **ginger-sesame broccoli**

1 teaspoon grated ginger (1/2-inch piece gingerroot)

1/4 cup water

3 cups packed broccoli florets

1/2 teaspoon toasted sesame oil

1. Finely grate enough ginger to measure 1 teaspoon.

2. In a medium microwave-safe bowl, stir together the water and ginger. Add the broccoli. Cover and microwave on High for 3 to 4 minutes, stirring once, until tender-crisp. Drain the water and return the broccoli to the bowl. Drizzle with the sesame oil. Cover to keep warm.

step 3

make the **mu shu roll-ups**

4 to 6 flour tortillas (10-inch diameter)

1/4 pound shiitake mushrooms

2 large scallions

6 large eggs

4 teaspoons vegetable oil

4 cups pre-shredded coleslaw mix

1/4 cup prepared garlic-and-ginger stir-fry sauce

Hoisin sauce for serving (optional)

1. Preheat the oven to 350°F. Wrap the tortillas in foil and place in the oven to heat.

2. Remove the stems from the mushrooms and thinly slice. Thinly slice the scallions.

3. Break the eggs into a medium bowl and beat with a fork to combine.

4. In a large (12-inch) nonstick skillet, heat 2 teaspoons of the vegetable oil over medium heat. Add the beaten eggs and cook, stirring frequently, for 1 to 2 minutes, or until softly scrambled. Transfer the eggs to a plate and cover loosely to keep warm.

5. Add the remaining 2 teaspoons vegetable oil to the skillet and heat until hot. Add the mushrooms and cook, stirring frequently, until softened. Add the coleslaw mix. Cook, stirring constantly, until tender-crisp, 1 to 2 minutes.

6. Stir in the stir-fry sauce and scallions and cook about 30 seconds to heat through. Remove the skillet from the heat and gently stir in the eggs.

step 4

serve

1. Place 1 warm tortilla on each plate. If desired, spread a little stir-fry sauce over the tortillas before filling or use hoisin sauce. Spoon the mu shu filling onto the center. Roll up the tortillas and serve with the broccoli as an accompaniment.

2. When ready for dessert, serve the orange sorbet sandwiches directly from the freezer.

Mu Shu Roll-Ups
Single serving is 1/4 of total recipe
CALORIES 456; PROTEIN 17g; CARBS 54g; TOTAL FAT 19g; SAT FAT 4g; CHOLESTEROL 319mg; SODIUM 598mg; FIBER 5g

soy, bean, and cheese burritos
tomato-avocado salad
seasonal fruit with strawberry sauce

menu gameplan

serves 4

shopping list

Monterey Jack cheese with jalapeños

Refrigerated soy crumbles

Black beans

Canned corn kernels

Chunky mild salsa

Flour tortillas (9- to 10-inch diameter)

Reduced-fat sour cream

Ripe tomato

Firm-ripe avocado

Cilantro

Lime (for juice)

Prewashed mixed salad greens

Frozen strawberries in syrup

from the salad bar

Red onion slices

Cut-up cantaloupe, honeydew, or pineapple
(or from the produce department)

from your pantry

Ground cumin

Olive oil

Salt and pepper

 Premade salsa and Monterey Jack cheese with jalapeños add lots of flavor to these burritos and help keep the ingredients list short, too.

beforeyoustart
Preheat the oven to 425°F to bake the burritos.

step 1 make the **soy, bean, and cheese burritos**

step 2 assemble the **tomato-avocado salad**

step 3 prepare the **seasonal fruit with strawberry sauce**

step 4 serve

"Making these burritos from scratch takes almost the same amount of time as heating up frozen ones! Sour cream and salsa keep them festive."

—minutemeals' Chef Sarah

step 1

make the **soy, bean, and cheese burritos**

1/4 pound Monterey Jack cheese with jalapeños

6 ounces refrigerated soy crumbles

1 can (15 ounces) black beans

1 cup drained canned corn kernels

1 jar (11 to 12 ounces) prepared chunky mild salsa

1 teaspoon ground cumin

4 burrito-size flour tortillas (9- to 10-inch diameter)

1/2 cup reduced-fat sour cream for serving

1. Preheat the oven to 425°F.

2. Finely dice the cheese. Cut the soy into 1/2-inch cubes, if necessary.

3. Rinse and drain the beans. Place the beans in a large (12-inch) non-stick skillet and mash about half of them with the back of a spoon. Add the corn, 1/2 cup of the salsa, the cumin, and soy crumbles. Cook, stirring frequently, over medium-high heat until hot, about 3 minutes. Remove the skillet from the heat.

4. Lay the tortillas on the work surface. Spoon the filling in a strip along the bottom of each tortilla, dividing it evenly. Sprinkle with the diced cheese. Roll each tortilla up partway, fold in the ends, and roll up to enclose the filling.

5. Place the tortillas, seam side down, on a cookie sheet. Bake for 10 minutes, or until hot.

step 2

assemble the **tomato-avocado salad**

1 ripe tomato

1 small firm-ripe avocado

1/4 cup red onion slices (1 small red onion)

1/4 cup loosely packed cilantro leaves

1 tablespoon fresh lime juice (1 lime)

1 tablespoon olive oil

Salt and pepper to taste

2 cups prewashed mixed salad greens

1. Rinse the tomato, pat dry, and cut into chunks. Pit, peel, and cut the avocado into chunks. Thinly slice enough red onion to measure 1/4 cup. Remove enough cilantro leaves from the sprigs to measure 1/4 cup. Squeeze the lime to measure 1 tablespoon juice.

2. In a medium bowl, combine the tomato, avocado, red onion, cilantro, lime juice, and olive oil. Season with salt and pepper. Mound the salad greens on top. Place the bowl on the table.

step 3

prepare the **seasonal fruit with strawberry sauce**

1 package (10 ounces) frozen strawberries in syrup

2 cups cut-up cantaloupe, honeydew, or pineapple

1. Thaw the strawberries in the microwave according to the directions on the package.

2. In a medium bowl, stir together the thawed strawberries and their syrup with the cut-up fruit. Refrigerate until serving time.

step 4

serve

1. Serve the burritos with the sour cream and remaining salsa on the side.

2. Toss the salad at the table, and serve it alongside the burritos.

3. When ready for dessert, spoon the fruit and some of the sauce into 4 dessert bowls and serve.

Soy, Bean, and Cheese Burritos
Single serving is 1/4 of total recipe
CALORIES 537; PROTEIN 29g; CARBS 68g; TOTAL FAT 19g; SAT FAT 10g; CHOLESTEROL 46mg; SODIUM 1496mg; FIBER 10g

two-alarm chili
cheesy biscuits
orange cream sorbet bars

serves 4

shopping list

Buttermilk baking mix such as Bisquick®

Pre-shredded sharp Cheddar cheese

Cornmeal

Green pepper slices (from the salad bar)

Pinto beans

Chunky chili-style diced or stewed tomatoes

Refrigerated soy crumbles

Reduced-fat sour cream (optional)

Orange cream sorbet bars

from your pantry

Vegetable cooking spray

Cayenne pepper

Skim milk

Vegetable oil

Chili powder

Vegetable broth (optional)

Salt and pepper

Hot sauce (optional)

beforeyoustart

Preheat the oven to 425°F to bake the biscuits.

step **1** make the **cheesy biscuits**

step **2** cook the **two-alarm chili**

step **3** serve

heads**up**
Soy crumbles sometimes come flavored with taco or Italian seasonings. Use the taco-flavored ones here, if you like, then adjust the seasonings in the chili to taste.

"This tastes as if it has been simmered for a long time. With both soy crumbles and beans, it's an excellent source of lean protein!"

—minutemeals' Chef Sarah

step 1

make the **cheesy biscuits**

Vegetable cooking spray

2$1/2$ cups buttermilk baking mix, such as Bisquick®

1 cup pre-shredded sharp Cheddar cheese

3 tablespoons cornmeal

$1/4$ teaspoon cayenne pepper

1 cup skim milk

1. Preheat the oven to 425°F. Spray a large cookie sheet with cooking spray.

2. In a medium bowl, stir together the baking mix, Cheddar, cornmeal, and cayenne. Add the milk and stir with a fork until a soft dough forms.

3. Drop biscuits by heaping tablespoons onto the prepared baking sheet, about 2 inches apart, making 12 biscuits. Bake for 10 to 12 minutes, or until golden brown. With a spatula, transfer the biscuits from the cookie sheet to a napkin-lined basket and serve warm.

step 2

cook the **two-alarm chili**

1 cup green pepper slices

1 can (15 ounces) pinto beans

1 tablespoon vegetable oil

1 tablespoon chili powder

1 can (14$1/2$ ounces) chunky chili-style diced or stewed tomatoes

1 package (12 ounces) refrigerated soy crumbles

$1/2$ cup vegetable broth or water

Salt and pepper to taste

Hot sauce for serving (optional)

Reduced-fat sour cream for serving (optional)

1. Chop the pepper slices. Rinse and drain the pinto beans.

2. In a large (12-inch) nonstick skillet, cook the chopped peppers in the vegetable oil over medium heat until slightly softened, about 2 minutes. Stir in the chili powder, undrained tomatoes, and beans.

3. Break the soy crumbles into the skillet, stir in the broth or water, and cover. Bring to a boil, reduce the heat to low, and simmer, covered, for 8 minutes. Season with salt and pepper.

step 3

serve

1. Serve the chili in bowls with the biscuits, or serve it over the biscuits, with any or all of the garnishes, if desired.

2. When ready for dessert, serve the sorbet bars directly from the freezer.

Two-Alarm Chili
Single serving is $1/4$ of total recipe
CALORIES 226; PROTEIN 24g; CARBS 26;
TOTAL FAT 5g; SAT FAT 0g; CHOLESTEROL 0mg;
SODIUM 1194mg; FIBER 10g

microwave savory stuffed peppers

green salad with parmesan and walnuts

tiramisù sundaes

serves 4

shopping list

Red, green, or yellow peppers

Marinara sauce with mushrooms and olives or pesto flavored

Instant brown rice

Refrigerated soy crumbles

Prewashed spinach leaves

Pre-shredded part-skim mozzarella

Prewashed Italian-style mixed salad greens

Walnut pieces

Pre-shredded Parmesan cheese

Packaged ladyfingers

Semisweet chocolate

Tiramisù gelato or coffee ice cream

from your pantry

Dried Italian seasoning

Vinaigrette dressing, store-bought or homemade

Salt and pepper

step 1   make the **microwave savory stuffed peppers**

step 2   assemble the **salad**

step 3   assemble the **tiramisù sundaes**

step 4   **serve**

headsup

Rotating the baking dish in the microwave helps to cook the pepper halves more evenly.

"Stuffed peppers are a family favorite. This updated version uses soy crumbles, which have no fat and over 10 grams of soy protein per serving."

—minutemeals' Chef Sarah

step 1

make the **microwave savory stuffed peppers**

4 small red, green, or yellow peppers

2 cups prepared marinara sauce with mushrooms and olives or pesto-flavored

3/4 cup water

1/2 cup instant brown rice

1 teaspoon dried Italian seasoning

1 package (12 ounces) refrigerated soy crumbles

2 cups packed prewashed spinach leaves

1 1/2 cups pre-shredded part-skim mozzarella cheese

Salt and pepper to taste

1. Halve, seed, and core each pepper.

2. Spread 1 cup of the marinara sauce in a microwave-safe 3-quart baking dish. Arrange the pepper halves, cut sides down, in the dish. Cover with a piece of waxed paper. Microwave on High, rotating the dish once, for 10 minutes, or until the peppers soften.

3. While the peppers are cooking, bring the water to a boil in a medium skillet. Stir in the rice and Italian seasoning. Add the soy crumbles and break them up with a spoon. Reduce the heat, cover and simmer for 8 minutes. Remove the skillet from the heat.

4. Stir 1/2 cup of the marinara sauce, the spinach, and 1 cup of the mozzarella into the rice mixture. Season with salt and pepper and stir until well combined. Turn the pepper halves over and spoon the filling into each of them. Drizzle the remaining marinara sauce over the peppers and sprinkle with the remaining 1/2 cup mozzarella. Microwave on High for 4 to 5 minutes, or until the peppers are hot.

step 2

assemble the **green salad with parmesan and walnuts**

1 bag (about 10 ounces) prewashed Italian-style mixed salad greens

1/4 cup walnut pieces

2 tablespoons pre-shredded Parmesan cheese

2 to 3 tablespoons prepared vinaigrette

Salt and pepper to taste

Place the salad greens, walnuts, and Parmesan in a large salad bowl. Add the vinaigrette and salt and pepper. Place the bowl on the table.

step 3

assemble the **tiramisù sundaes**

8 packaged ladyfingers

1/2 ounce semisweet chocolate

1 pint tiramisu gelato or coffee ice cream

1. Place 2 ladyfingers in each of 4 dessert dishes.

2. Grate the chocolate and reserve.

step 4

serve

1. Serve the stuffed peppers directly from the baking dish.

2. Toss the salad at the table, and serve it alongside the peppers, or on separate salad plates.

3. When ready for dessert, scoop gelato over the ladyfingers in each bowl, sprinkle with some of the grated chocolate, and serve.

Microwave Savory Stuffed Peppers
Single serving is 1/4 of total recipe
CALORIES 342; PROTEIN 32g; CARBS 33g;
TOTAL FAT 10g; SAT FAT 5g; CHOLESTEROL 25mg;
SODIUM 1609mg; FIBER 10g

a

Agrodolce, glazed green beans, 28–29

À la Mexicana, dulce de leche ice cream, 102–3

À la mode

    brownies, 56–57

    peach pie, 126–27

À la Provençale, cod, 104–5

Alfredo, tonnato, with sun-dried tomatoes, 118–19

Almond

    biscotti, store-bought, 76–77

    cookies, store-bought, 78–79

    honey, gelato, 132–33

    pound cake delight, 124–25

Amaretti cookies, store-bought, 118–19

    crumbled, peach coupes with, 148–49

Ambrosial Pineapple, 58–59

Angel Hair Pasta, 112–13

Antipasto Salad, 128–29, 136–37

Apple(s)

    cider, spiced, warm, 68–69

    crisp, 64–65

    -pecan slaw, 158–59

    turnovers, store-bought, 38–39

Applesauce and Oatmeal Raisin Cookies, store-bought, 16–17

Applesauce with Cinnamon and Honey, 42–43

Apricot glaze, broiled chicken with, 6–7

Artichoke and Olive Salad, 118–19

Arugula, Red Onion, and Black Olive Salad, 134–35

Asian Cucumber Salad, 34–35

Asian Orange Chicken, 12–13

Asian Pork and Noodles, 84–85

Asparagus with Shallot Butter, 6–7

Assorted Mustards, 42–43

Avocado

    Caesar Salad with Lime, 2–3

    mashed, 162–63

    orange and, salads, 102–3, 154–55

    tomato-, salad, 166–67

b

Bacon

    braised pork with onions and, 76–77

    chicken and, salad, hot, 18–19

    dressing, warm, 24–25

    and tomato pizzettes, 136–37

Baked Beans, store-bought, 42–43

Baked Salmon with Crunchy Mustard Crust, 98–99

Baklava, store-bought, 108–9

Balsamic-Basil Tomatoes, 20–21

Banana Splits, 138–39

Bananas foster sauce, vanilla ice cream with, 10–11

Barbecued Chicken Thighs, 16–17

Basil

    balsamic-, tomatoes, 20–21

    chicken and, sausages, grilled, 144–45

    fresh, sliced tomatoes with, 64–65

    in Giant Omelette, 160–61

    peaches and, sautéed turkey with, 22–23

    peas with roasted peppers, 116–17

    tomatoes and, on Romaine, 76–77

Basmati rice, 104–5, 110–11

    with cashews, 74–75

Basque Chicken, 8–9

Bean(s)

    baked, store-bought, 42–43

    in Beef, Ramen Noodle, and Vegetable Stew, 48–49

    canned, 140–45

    Drunken Beans, 144–45

    Mexican Tortilla Pizzas, 142–43

    Mini Rigatoni with Beans and Gazpacho Sauce, 140–41

    cumin-scented, 162–63

    drunken, 144–45

    green, 52–53

    green, buttered, 80–81

    green, glazed, agrodolce, 28–29

    green, potato, and turkey salad, 24–25

    pinto, mini rigatoni with, and gazpacho sauce, 140–41

    soy, and cheese burritos, 166–67

    white, pasta with sun-dried tomato pesto and, 122–23

Beef

    ground

        Beef, Ramen Noodle, and Vegetable Stew, 48–49

        Microwave Zucchini Boats with Mexican Beef Stuffing, 46–47

        Moroccan Beef and Squash with Couscous, 50–51

    steak

        Spicy Thai Beef on Crisp Salad, 54–55

        Steaks Pizzaiola, 52–53

        Steaks with Shallot and Herb Butter, 56–57

    stir-fry

        Beef Fajitas, 60–61

        Sesame Garlic Beef Stir-Fry, 58–59

        Sloppy Joes, 62–63

Beer

    in Cheddar Cheese Fondue, 158–59

    in Drunken Beans, 144–45

    in Turkey Sausage and Sauerkraut, 42–43

Berry(ies). *See also specific types*

    kiwi and, yogurt parfaits, 52–53

    lemon, cheesecakes, store-bought, 20–21

    yogurt, sliced strawberries with, store-bought, 18–19

Biscuits

    buttermilk, 36–37

    cheesy, 168–69

Biscotti, almond, store-bought, 76–77

Bittersweet Brownie Mousse, 22–23

Blondies, store-bought, 4–5, 80–81

Blueberries, honeyed cantaloupe with, 130–31

Braised Lamb Chops with Spring Vegetables, 88–89

Braised Pork with Bacon and Onions, 76–77